FOUND MONEY

FOUND MONEY

SIMPLE STRATEGIES FOR UNCOVERING
THE **HIDDEN PROFIT** AND
CASH FLOW IN YOUR
BUSINESS

STEVE WILKINGHOFF

WILEY

John Wiley & Sons, Inc.

Library of Congress Cataloging-in-Publication Data:

Wilkinghoff, Steve, 1969–
    Found money : simple strategies for uncovering the hidden profit and cash flow in your business/Steve Wilkinghoff.
        p.   cm.
    Includes bibliographical references.
    ISBN 978-0-470-48335-0 (cloth : acid-free paper)
        1. Industrial management.   2. Business enterprises.   3. Businesspeople.
    4. Profit.   I. Title.
    HD31.W5159 2009
    658.15'5–dc22

                                                                    2009004119

Printed in the United States of America

10 9 8 7 6 5 4 3 2 1

To Sherri, Julia, Lauryn, Graeme, and Carter.
You are the five best things in life,
and give me strength, motivation, and humor.
I love you all very much.

CONTENTS

Contents

ACKNOWLEDGMENTS

I would like to express my sincere and deep appreciation to the many people who have contributed, each in their unique way, to the realization of my vision for helping business owners throughout the world.

To my wife, Sherri, for being such a great and supportive friend, partner, and mother to our children. You make it possible for me to work, travel, create, and build my vision of transforming the lives of business owners throughout the world.

To my children, Julia, Lauryn, Graeme, and Carter. You four are proof that angels really do exist here on earth. I have a bottomless well of love and admiration for each of you in my heart.

To Mom, Dad, and Max. Thank you for your love, encouragement and support in all my dreams and all I've aspired to accomplish over the years.

To Michael Gerber. You are an amazing person with powerful insights into the world of business. And as a friend and mentor, you are absolutely wonderful to know.

Thank you all.

I am a reader of books. I am also an author of books. Over the last month, I have read more than 25 books. Over the past 25 years I have written 9 books. Like you, I suppose, I read—and I write—to be inspired, to be caught up in new worlds, to have my imagination piqued, to listen to the sound of words. But, most of all, I read and I write to be entranced by an incredibly well told story. I am infatuated with a great, original spin on an old story.

This book, *Found Money*, is just that: a great, original spin on an old story.

In this case, the old story is the story of money.

According to Steve Wilkinghoff, money is *not* the root of all evil; it's our lack of understanding of money that is.

As entrepreneurs and business owners, you and I are faced every day with the story of money as it plays its way in and out of our businesses and our lives.

As entrepreneurs and business owners, you and I have faced the dreaded meeting with our financial advisors, accountants, CPAs, CFOs, and, of course, with our husbands and wives.

Always, we are asked those dreaded questions: How did this happen? Why didn't we make any money? Why did sales not go up—or, even worse, why did sales go down?

And, most of all, where is the money when you need it?

In *Found Money*, Steve Wilkinghoff will tell you an old story in an original, compelling, and amazingly important way. He'll tell you that your CPA isn't your greatest friend, your Capital Advisor® is.

What is a Capital Advisor®?

According to Steve Wilkinghoff, a Capital Advisor® is a professional who has mastered the art and science of finding money in your company, long before you ever need it, and showing you why and how you can design your company in such a way as to create found money everywhere you look: in the Sales Department, in the Marketing Department, in the Production Division, in the Inventory Control System.

In short, Steve Wilkinghoff is the supreme Capital Advisor® for your business and your life.

He will show you in the pages of this book how to think about money in a way you never have before.

He will demonstrate to you in this book that the story of money is a magical story, one loaded with promise, one that always can have a happy ending ... if you approach it the way your Capital Advisor® shows you to. If you are determined to do more than add up the results at the end of the story, design those results at the beginning of the story, where every great company lives.

Enjoy this book.

Adopt its principles.

But, most of all, listen to Steve Wilkinghoff, one of the most important storytellers you have ever had the privilege to meet.

I did. And my life has never been the same since.

—MICHAEL E. GERBER
Author of *The E-Myth Revisited*,
Awakening the Entrepreneur Within,
and Founder and CEO of The
Entrepreneur Capital Corporation

Have you ever seen a small child trying to "walk" a large dog? Of course you have—we've all seen that familiar scene at least once before. A small child (heck, sometimes even a small adult) holds on to a leash with all his or her strength, teeth clenched and neck muscles popping from the exertion of trying to control the animal. The child tries to lead the dog in whatever direction he or she wants it to go, and the dog goes along with the child—as long as it wants to.

But the large dog is definitely the one who's really in control. That becomes obvious the second that dog picks up a scent, sees something it wants to explore, wants to go faster, or wants to go slower (yeah, right). Then it goes off in the direction it wants to go, and the small child is taken along with the dog.

It's those moments where it becomes obvious that the dog is really the one in control. Up until that point, the child might have felt that he or she was in control, but that was just an illusion that continued as long as the dog went along with the child. When the dog shows who's really in control, though, the child more or less goes along for the ride. The child holds on, hoping the dog will eventually get to where the child wants it to go.

Sadly, an awful lot of business owners have that exact same relationship with their business. They have the illusion that they are in control and their business is going where they want it to go. However, that control is an illusion. When the business demonstrates that *it* is the one in control, the owner is pulled along wherever the business goes. The owner holds on, teeth clenched, and hopes that eventually they will get wherever it is they hope to end up—safely, with at least some dignity, and not totally wiped out.

The relationship between many business owners and their businesses became very apparent when a tougher economic environment reared its head. Suddenly, confident, successful business owners who thought they had things under control realized they weren't really in control at all.

But the great news is that the business owner doesn't have to be yanked along by events. No matter how your business environment changes, the fundamentals remain unchanged. A business still must do three things (at the same time) to make any money for its owner. Products and services must each meet three criteria (at the same time) to make money for the business and the owner. And customers must each meet three criteria (at the same time) to make money for the business and its owner.

Knowing those things gives the business owners *real control*, rather than the illusion of control. And that means the owners can make appropriate decisions in any economic environment. In tough economic times, that knowledge can be used to defend the business in a way that preserves precious capital while still making money for the owner and the company's employees. In prosperous economic times, that knowledge enables the owners to grow their businesses in a way that is sound and sustainable and still makes money.

We've all heard some (usually all) of the comments below. In fact, if you're a business owner, you've probably said them yourself:

- Our customers aren't buying right now.

- No one can get credit to run their business.

- I'm just swamped here in this business.

- I haven't had a real day off in weeks (months, years, etc.).

- I probably could make just as much, without the stress and hassles, if I went to work for someone else.

- I just can't seem to get ahead.

- If I could get more customers, I'd be doing great.

This is an ultra short list. If you and I really tried hard to remember every similar comment we've ever heard, or said, the list could go on for days (but that wouldn't really be all that fun, it would waste our time, and I don't want to steal your thunder for your next party).

The point is this. Despite the huge potential out there, the relationships most business owners have with their businesses are broken. Most business owners are feeling incredibly frustrated, helpless, lost, and fed up. They are working harder than ever, having a tougher financial time than ever, feeling more helpless than ever, and definitely not getting the dream lifestyle they once had envisioned from their business.

And they are so very frustrated because their efforts never seem to result in them getting ahead. They often find themselves being forced to work harder, and harder, and harder, and harder, just to keep from sliding backwards.

The simple, but sad, truth is that their businesses are in control of them and their lives. The business sets the pace. The business decides when (or if) the owner can get away from it to spend time with family, friends, and interests. The business decides how much fun and free time they get. The business decides how much money the owner gets (or, as is often the case, how much money the owner must spend on the business!).

If that sounds depressing, that's because it is!

The vast majority of business owners are literally enslaved by their businesses. They have allowed themselves to become servants to their businesses, rather than the other way around. Many business owners are feeling so beat up and so emotionally drained by their business that, given the chance, they would quit the business—or at least seriously consider it.

If they could find someone to take over their businesses, pay off their debts, and let them break even, they'd be out of there. But who the heck would buy their business? Who, in their right mind, would pay ANYTHING just so they could take the business owner's place and start suffering so the owner wouldn't have to?

Let's just assume, for a moment, that a business owner happened to find some freak out there who *would* buy his or her business and allow the owner to break even (i.e., clear debts, etc.).

When you consider that:

- Breaking even means that all the owner receives for his or her years of hard work is the wage they managed to earn while owning the business.

- Many business owners end up taking wages that are less than the market value for their effort, talents, AND RISK, which means that the owner wouldn't really break even at all.

In fact, the owner would come out way behind. Tragically, if the owner sells out to "break even" and has taken a wage less than market value (which seems to be quite common), then the owner has managed to *destroy wealth* over their years of ownership.

These owners destroyed wealth because they would have been better off if they had worked that hard for someone else and been paid market value for their efforts. But instead, while they poured their emotions, money, and energy into the business, sacrificing family time and so many other things, these owners were actually making themselves worse off financially than if they had never started the business.

Why is that?

The sad, but simple, answer is that an awful lot of business owners don't really understand how their business makes money. Sure, they may know "intellectually" how net profit is defined. They may even know how to read their financial statements.

But that doesn't mean they understand how their business makes them money.

You see, how a business actually makes money is an entirely different thing than simply reading a set of financial statements. And if a business owner doesn't understand how the business makes money, it's *impossible* for that owner to *control* how much money gets created, or the specific way the business goes about doing it.

And that puts the owner under the control of the business—the complete opposite of the way things are supposed to be.

The good news is that this situation, while exceedingly common, is absolutely fixable.

And that's what this book is all about—giving you (the business owner) the knowledge, tools, and motivation to get control of your business, get the profit, fun, and free time you want, and consistently and reliably *create* the financial result you want, so that you can live your dream lifestyle.

Over the years, I have had the privilege of working with hundreds of different businesses, conducting endless hours of research, and I have had many intimate discussions with the owners (and their loved ones) of a staggering variety of businesses. All that experience, research, and learning has always led back to a recurring theme—most business owners who struggle do so because they don't understand *how* their business truly makes money for them (and how it *should* do that).

Despite some vast differences in industries, operations, strategies, and tactics, all those businesses have been exactly the same at their core. And that means the same set of principles, knowledge, and tactics work for every business, no matter what size, what industry, or what economic environment.

This book builds on that fact. It gives you the knowledge (in a simple and understandable form) and tactics to shine the core of your business until it gleams, until your business is transformed into a powerful vehicle that will take you to your dream lifestyle allowing you to enjoy your life to the fullest.

This book will be your guide to finding all the profit and cash flow that is hidden in your business, that is hidden in it right now, and that has probably always been hiding right in front of you.

So let's get started.

FOUND MONEY

CHAPTER

1

WHAT'S THE PURPOSE OF YOUR BUSINESS?

In my experience with hundreds of business owners over the last 15 years, I've realized that many, many of them are confused. They don't really understand the purpose of their business, why it exists. And because of that, they do things, or allow things, that just don't make sense.

Building, maintaining, and keeping a successful business, of any size, depends on a crystal-clear picture of what a business is supposed to do. So let's jump right in and look at the answer to the most important question you can *ever* ask yourself as a business owner.

WHAT DO *YOU* THINK IS THE PURPOSE OF YOUR BUSINESS?

Every time I ask this question at seminars or when working with a new client, a certain pattern is reinforced. After years of asking this question, I've heard a list of answers that are repeated so

1

often I have come to expect them. The answers are usually some variation of one of the following:

- We make a difference in people's lives.

- I love what I do, and wanted to make a living at it.

- I wanted to be rewarded for how hard I worked.

- We help people.

- We provide a valuable product or service to people.

- I like to make my customers happy.

- I enjoy improving my customers' lives.

- People need what we sell.

- I can't imagine doing anything else.

- I have a hard time working for someone else.

- I enjoy being in control of my future.

Every single one of those answers and their many variations are examples of wonderful goals and beliefs. But when it comes to a reason for any business to exist, they are all completely . . .

. . . WRONG!

Now don't misunderstand me and think I'm a heartless jerk. Those things are all very noble and wonderful, and I think they are all great things to want to do and accomplish. I'm certainly not belittling them or saying they aren't worthwhile ambitions. In fact, it's because people want to do those things that the world is made better. Just think about what kind of place our world would be if people didn't think like that.

All those reasons are beautiful, loving, and passionate ideas that speak to a higher purpose. But when it comes to a reason for your business to exist, they are completely *wrong*! Not a single one of those responses is the reason your business exists. They just don't cut it.

After all, if you simply want to make a difference in people's lives, you can find ready work in the teaching profession, the ministries, or one of many other professions and vocations. There are lots of careers that provide wonderful opportunities to make a difference in people's lives. If that's your goal, you don't need to own a business to accomplish it. Wanting to make a difference isn't a reason for your business to exist (although, again, it's a great goal to have).

If you simply want to enjoy what you do and make a living, there's an infinite variety of jobs out there that will let your talent shine. And you'll be able to shine without the risk, stress, and extra workload that comes with owning your own business. So that's not a good enough answer either.

Looking to be rewarded for how hard you work? Again, you can do that with far less stress and risk by working for someone else. Just make sure you do it in one of the almost-limitless commission sales positions or similar positions where your compensation is directly linked to your results. So that's not a good enough answer, is it?

Providing a valuable product or service isn't the answer either. There are many jobs and businesses out there that could give you the opportunity to provide things people really value. For example, think how lucky we are to have all the nurses who work so hard in the medical community. They provide an absolutely vital service (in fact, they provide a service that's priceless), yet don't do it as a business. It's their profession.

And, hey, if you really just want to be in control of your time and income, you can accomplish that in any number of ways that don't require you to have your own business. In fact, the wildly popular book *The 4-Hour Workweek*, by Timothy Ferriss, has tons of great advice about how to control your time and income—even while working for someone else.

But I'm Not Heartless!

Now before you start thinking I'm advocating a business that is cold and heartless, let me get something straight. I'm not, for one moment, saying these things aren't important. And I'm not saying they aren't worthy goals. Not at all.

In fact, I truly believe those thoughts and goals are part of what make our spiritual and business lives rich and rewarding. Having objectives like that to aim for is wonderful. They are great ambitions to aspire to and want to accomplish.

And I'm not saying you have to change who you are or what you believe. Well, actually I *am* saying that you most likely will have to change some of what you believe. But that's only because you probably have some incorrect and very limiting beliefs about your business. And we'll work to change those—in a good way.

What I am saying is that the reasons listed previously for being in business, or similar ones, are *not* satisfactory reasons for your business to exist. And if you fall into the trap of thinking that any of them *are* the reason it exists, one of two things will happen, neither good:

1. You get trapped in a hellish lifestyle, in which you work way too hard in your business and simply manage to make a living—just getting by. You sacrifice your physical and emotional health, as well as important relationships with your family and friends. You struggle to get everything done that needs doing, and no matter how hard you work you just never seem to get quite caught up.

   You end up overworked, stressed, unhappy, unhealthy, and burned out. And the worst part is that, for all your efforts, you don't even generate any real wealth for yourself and your family. You end up with nothing more than a "job" that you've created for yourself. And it's the worst kind of job. It gives you a low-paying position (in fact, often below minimum wage for the hours you devote), a punishing workload, almost unlimited risk, and little (if any) freedom or flexibility to get away to relax, enjoy yourself, and connect with your family and friends.

2. Even worse, you discover that despite your worthy goals (helping others, etc.) your business simply isn't viable. No

matter how hard you seem to work, it doesn't make enough money or cash flow to continue operating.

So, despite your desire to help others and provide them with something of value, your business simply can't sustain itself. You end up putting more and more money into the business; eroding more and more of your wealth and personal net worth as time goes on. In the end, you may even be forced to close your doors, end up working in a job you may not like, and suffer emotional and financial damage.

It's clear that neither of those scenarios is fun, profitable, or good for your financial and emotional health, nor for your family and loved ones.

SO WHAT *IS* THE PURPOSE OF YOUR BUSINESS?

To make money. End of story.

Really. That's it. The answer is that simple.

Now, I don't want to sound like a heartless mercenary (though I'm certainly willing to do so if that's what it takes to make my point), but *making money* really and truly is the only reason your business exists. It might sound harsh, but it's the honest truth. Get over it.

Of course, it goes without saying (but I'm going to say it anyway) that your business needs to make money honestly, ethically, and legally.

Let me explain myself. The reason your business exists to make money is that everything else comes from that one thing. It's only after your business makes money for you that you have *options* to do what you want with your money and your time.

Once you've created a business that actually makes money, you can do one, some, or all of the following:

- Help people by using the money your business makes

- Help more people by expanding your business

5

- Work less by hiring some talented team members to continue running the business so that it keeps making money when you're not there

- Travel

- Increase your skills and knowledge in your area of expertise

- Develop a new area of expertise

- Do whatever else you desire in your dream lifestyle

Owning a business is a lot like being given a raw piece of wood and some carving tools. If you take the time to learn the skills you need to effectively use the tools, and you apply them, you can transform that piece of wood into whatever you envision.

But just looking at the piece of wood and tools, using the tools poorly or improperly, or just wishing for a certain finished result isn't going to do anything for you. If that's all you do, you will never get anywhere near the place you'd really like to be.

Here's a real-life example for you.

A man named Bill Austin started a company called Starkey Laboratories. This company has grown into a global technology business that manufactures some of the finest hearing aids, with the most advanced technology, in the world.

Bill has always had a passion for helping people achieve the gift of hearing. And a huge part of that passion manifested itself in Bill's creation of a foundation that provides hearing aids to underprivileged people around the world—people who would otherwise never be touched by the gift of hearing.

I've been to one of Bill's fundraising galas, and the emotions that are part of his missions around the world are something you'll never forget. You can't help but be deeply moved and changed by his amazing foundation (The Starkey Hearing Foundation, www.sotheworldmayhear.org) and its wonderful work.

But let's get one thing clear. Bill's passion for helping those who truly need his love could *never* have been realized as effectively if he hadn't first built a business that creates enough money for him to advance the work of his foundation. If Bill had simply thought of himself as selling hearing aids, he'd still be helping people. There's no doubt about that. But he would only be helping people who could come to his clinic and afford his services.

And if he were still doing that, as great as that would be, he wouldn't be fulfilling his dream lifestyle, nor would he be changing lives and giving the gift of hearing to people in underdeveloped nations around the globe.

In fact, by building a business that made money so he could pursue his dream lifestyle, Bill (through his foundation[1]) has been able to provide, since the year 2000 alone, more than 310,000 hearing aids to needy people across the globe.

That's the power of creating a business that makes enough money and provides the profit and cash flow you desire to create your dream lifestyle. If Bill Austin hadn't got the order right, he would have been lucky to help a handful of people. But because he understood that to do his foundation work, he first had to have a business that made money, he now helps thousands of people receive the gift of hearing *every year*.

THE FOUND MONEY SYSTEM CAN HELP

If the purpose of a business is to make money, it's an absolute tragedy that most businesses are allowed to run *as if that's not the purpose at all*. In fact, many businesses seem to be run as if the owners are afraid of making money, or that it's a bad thing. But as the example of Bill Austin and the Starkey Foundation clearly demonstrate, making money is the best way for a business owner to be able to help others.

I hope I've convinced you, because your success and your personal, financial, and emotional health depend on it. Your business needs to be run so that it will make money—as much money as it can, legally, ethically, and morally. That is what will give you the power to help others, change lives and maybe even change the world.

---

[1] Starkey Hearing Foundation, www.sotheworldmayhear.org.

The knowledge and tools in this book can help you get there. So promise yourself that you'll work through this book, internalize what it teaches, and take action on what you find.

FIVE KEYS TO SUCCESS WITH THE FOUND MONEY SYSTEM

Your success with the knowledge and tools in this book will depend on five fundamental traits. Understanding and practicing these traits allows you to plan, launch, and sustain a successful Found Money system in your business that will create more profit and cash flow than you may have thought possible. The following traits aren't just words to read. Pause and think about each one and how you can apply it in your business.

1. *Commitment.* It's a simple truth that commitment, layered on top of even basic activities, will create much more profit, cash flow, fun, and free time than a series of technically superior ideas which you never consistently follow up on or implement.

   Ensure you are committed to following through with developing and implementing your Found Money system. Promise yourself. Make a sincere commitment that you will take the necessary actions to create the new levels of profit, cash flow, and free time that are waiting in your business right now.

2. *Investment.* Your Found Money efforts are an investment, not a drain. The Found Money system requires a minimal investment of money; instead, the real key is your willingness and desire to invest your time, energy, and creativity.

   No matter how busy you may be (or think you are) right now, commit to applying an open mind and investing your time, effort and creativity in this process. Whatever of these you invest in your business, you are most definitely going to get back in a huge multiple. In fact, it is the absolute best investment available on the planet today.

3. *Consistency*. Learning and applying the Found Money system, thinking, and tools will likely require some changes in your mindset and the way you have historically done things in your business. That means, essentially, that you are going to be replacing some old habits with new ones. As with any new habit, it will take a while for them to become ingrained and replace the old ones.

   If you aren't consistent in your actions, you won't be able to get the maximum potential that is waiting for you.

4. *Open-Mindedness*. You *must* resolve to be open-minded to some nontraditional ways of thinking about your business, your customers, and the roles of each. If you aren't open-minded, you will be tempted to ignore parts of the Found Money system or try to "cherry-pick" only certain parts of it. You will still get some benefits if you do that, but they will fall far short of the true potential for your business (and your dream lifestyle).

   Just because something has always been done a certain way doesn't mean there isn't a better way just waiting to be discovered and used.

5. *Testing*. The great thing about the Found Money system is that it allows you to (in fact strongly encourages you to) test everything before making any major changes or decisions that permanently affect your business.

   This goes along with being open-minded. By testing continuously and passionately, you can drive your business in a continual upward spiral of increasing profit and cash flow, and create some absolutely stunning changes and improvements in your lifestyle in the process. Testing is the key to achieving these changes and improvements with limited (or often zero) risk to your business. Such is the power of adopting a testing mindset.

So now that you understand the purpose of your business and the five traits needed to cultivate true success with the Found Money system and tools, Chapter 2 will take a look at the things that must happen for your business to fulfill its purpose and make money for you.

2

WHEN DOES YOUR BUSINESS MAKE MONEY?

That's really *the* question for every business owner, isn't it? After all, at the end of each day, week, month, and year, if it's to be successful, a business *must* make money. It must make enough money to repay its debts, re-invest in more growth, sustain its operations, and pay the owners enough to live their desired lifestyle.

If a business doesn't make enough money to accomplish all four of these things, it's an absolute failure. That may sound harsh, but it's really not. Don't stop reading. Keep going, and you'll see exactly what I mean.

A NASTY URBAN LEGEND

Unfortunately, a bit of an urban legend has developed over the years that says a business is a failure only if it can't repay its debts and can't repay other creditors. But that myth leaves the

11

owner out of the picture and leaves them taking whatever is left over—essentially waiting for some crumbs to fall from the table.

That's just so wrong. I take a strong stand on this one, and I'll say it again: If your business doesn't make enough money to allow you to live your desired lifestyle and maximize its profit and cash flow—it's a *failure*! Yes, of course any business must also pay its creditors and lenders if it is to avoid failure; I'm not disputing that. What I am saying is that the business also owes a "debt" to its *owners*, and that debt needs to be treated just as seriously, and with just as much vigor, as a debt to any other creditor.

Sadly, it seems that most businesses don't let their owners create their desired lifestyle. Most business owners are being controlled (and having their lifestyles controlled) by their business. And that means, according to my definition, most businesses are failures.

There's good news, though. Most businesses' state of failure can be changed quite easily. The way to change it is for the business owner to become knowledgeable about how to *create* the financial results he or she wants from the business. And the way to start that process is to develop a solid understanding of the basics.

Like everything in life, knowing the basics is a necessary foundation toward mastery. Once you know the basics of the Found Money system, you can start working toward mastery of your business, transforming both it and your life.

You see, once you know how your business makes money, you can make decisions to control *how* it makes that money, and *how much* money it makes. You will have an almost unlimited range of options for creating a business to serve your dream lifestyle.

Over the years, however, I have discovered that an awful lot of business owners simply don't know and don't understand how their business really makes money. It's not their fault. It's just that they have never been shown the basic fundamentals of how their business does that.

I have found this lack of understanding to be the case with new business owners as well as very successful business owners who have been in business for years. In many cases, the success of the business and its owners came as a result of a tremendous amount of hard work (usually much more than would have been necessary if financial results were created differently), or by being in the right place at the right time.

While those methods of succeeding are certainly welcome when they occur, they still mean that the business is in control of the owner. When economic times get tougher, the business owner is left with nothing else to do but "hunker down" and ride it out, because they don't know what actions need to be taken.

It's not the business owner's fault. I'm not saying that for a second. After all, this system isn't taught in most schools, colleges, or universities. The vast majority of accountants don't understand it, either; they are trained to report on historical earnings and their accuracy, not deal proactively with an ongoing business.

But because the business owners haven't learned (and haven't been shown) how their businesses actually make money, most of them, and their businesses, are helplessly adrift. They are forced to rely on luck, the economy, and their competitors for their success.

Understanding How Your Business Makes Money Is Different Than Just Reading Your Financial Statements

You might be able to read and understand a financial statement (although many business owners can't, because they have never been shown). But that doesn't mean you necessarily understand how your business makes money.

It's a lot like trying to read a legal document or tax legislation. It's all written in English (or whatever local language is appropriate). But that does not mean you truly *understand* the information contained in those documents, even if you can *read* every single word.

Whenever I give seminars or coach business owners, I find that they almost always fall into one of two categories:

1. They don't know how their business makes them money, and they admit it.

2. They think they know how their business makes them money, but their beliefs are wrong (and potentially harmful).

I have met a few business owners over the years who really and truly do "get it"—business owners who really understand how their business makes money for them. In those rare cases, the business owner has always learned it from a mentor or successful family member who has passed the knowledge on to them.

That's what this book is going to do for you. It will become *your* mentor, showing you what the "lucky few" have been shown already. And you will be able to put yourself in control of where your business is going, the financial results it creates, and the ways it's going to do that.

HOW *DOESN'T* YOUR BUSINESS MAKE MONEY?

Before we get to the part about how your business makes money, let's take a quick look at some of the common *misconceptions* about how it does that—some more urban legends. I've heard each of these, in many different forms, from many, many different business owners over the years, spoken as though they are the complete truth. I'm going to discuss each of them below, because they are so prevalent, yet oh, so wrong. And I will show you why they are so wrong.

Moneymaking Myth #1

A business makes money when it sells something.

An awful lot of businesses around the globe sell a lot of stuff. And many of those businesses, even though they sell a lot of stuff, still don't make any money. For example, let's look at the satellite radio company XM Satellite. In the three months that ended in September 2007, this company had revenue of

$287 million.[1] Clearly, it sold something (in fact, it sold an awful lot of "somethings"—satellite radios and subscriptions to its programming). But guess what? In that same period, despite selling $287 million worth of "somethings," the company lost money. Its loss for those three months totaled $145 million.[2]

Simply selling something, then, isn't the way your business makes money.

Moneymaking Myth #2

A business makes money when it attracts a new customer.

As the XM Satellite example shows, simply attracting customers is no guarantee of making money, either.

In fact, a study by the consulting firms Bain & Company and Mainspring showed that in online consumer electronic sales, *only 24% of customers are actually profitable.*[3] Read that again and think about it for a few moments.

That is an absolutely shocking statistic!

It means over *three-quarters (76%)* of customers of those retailers *don't* make the companies any money. And it's not just that they don't make the companies any money—based on businesses I have worked with over the years, the odds are extremely high that they actually *lose* money for the companies.

In other words, the money the companies make on the 24% of their customers who are profitable has to make up for the

---

[1]"XM Satellite Radio Holdings Inc. Announces Third Quarter 2007 Results." Press Release dated October 25, 2007, retrieved from http://xmradio.mediaroom.com/index.php?s=press_releases&item=1524.

[2]"XM Satellite Radio Holdings Inc. Announces Third Quarter 2007 Results." Press Release dated October 25, 2007, retrieved from http://xmradio.mediaroom.com/index.php?s=press_releases&item=1524.

[3]Bain & Company and Mainspring."Few Online Retail Customer Segments Are Profitable, Study Finds; Bain & Company, Mainspring Show Profitable Segments Linked to Acquisition Channels and Business Models." Business Wire.Article dated March 30, 2000; retrieved from http://findarticles.com/p/articles/mi_m0EIN/is_2000_March_30/ai_60956465.

losses incurred from the other 76% of their customers before the company as a whole makes a dime!

Consider that for a moment. Let the implication really sink in.

That statistic says that more than three-quarters of a company's customers dig a financial hole. And then the business must work like crazy to fill that hole with profit earned on the remaining quarter of their customers, *just to break even*. It's only once the "financial hole" has been filled that the business can actually start making money—what a waste of effort!

In other words, the companies in the study would have made more money if they didn't have 76% of their customers! They wouldn't have had a financial hole to fill, and all the money from the profitable customers would have gone toward increasing the businesses' financial results (rather than having to use part of it to repair the damage caused by the unprofitable 76%).

Clearly then, simply attracting new customers is the not the magic answer to making money. And as you'll discover later in this book, attracting the wrong customer could actually be the worst thing possible for your business.

Moneymaking Myth #3

A business makes money when it comes up with a wonderful new product or service.

Let's look at a company called ALR Technologies. This company has developed a great product: a special "medication reminder" designed for people who have chronic medical conditions and need medication on a regular basis. It sounds like a great product. And it definitely serves a great purpose.

But the company hasn't made any money yet.

In fact, during 2007, the company continued to generate net losses and use up more cash than it created.[4] At the time I'm writing this, without the continued support of its investors and

---

[4]"Quarterly Report Pursuant to Section 13 or 15(d) of the Securities Exchange Act of 1934 for the Quarterly Period Ended September 30, 2007—Form 10-QSB," as filed with the United States Securities and Exchange Commission.

creditors, there is some question about the company's ability to continue operations.

So simply creating a wonderful product isn't the answer either.

Moneymaking Myth #4

A business makes money when it comes up with a great marketing campaign.

Several years ago, a new company, mapsworldwide.com, was started with the vision of selling specialty maps to people around the world—maps for hikers, pilots, sailors, fishermen, and so on.

The man who started the company had experience in public relations. He knew the mechanics of creating a dynamite marketing campaign very well. His marketing was no doubt great. It included professional artwork, targeted audiences, targeted mailings, great copy, and all the other elements that make for what is usually considered to be great marketing.

Based on the wonderful marketing plan, the business went out and spent over $40,000 on its marketing campaign. The money went quickly, and according to the founder, had no effect whatsoever on his business.[5]

HOW *DOES* YOUR BUSINESS MAKE MONEY?

Ahhhhh, now we're asking the million-dollar question.

After all, making money is the reason for your business to exist, right? And because of that, you need to know how it makes money, so you can gain control over the process of creating the financial results you want.

For your business to make money, it must do three things. And it must do them all at the same time.

---

[5]Norris, Sue. "Marketing Campaigns That Lose Their Way." The Guardian. Article dated September 29, 2005; retrieved from www.guardian.co.uk/technology/2005/sep/29/businesssense.businesssense6.

TO MAKE MONEY, YOUR BUSINESS MUST:

1. Generate a positive net profit

2. Give you an adequate return on investment

3. Generate a strong enough positive cash flow

We'll cover each of these three things in more detail in the next section on the Triple Overlap. For now, I want you to get used to thinking about your business doing all three of these things, and doing them all at the same time.

Too often, business owners fall into the trap of thinking their business only needs to do *one* of these three things for it to make money. It's like they become mesmerized into thinking they can pick one of the three elements, focus their attention on that one element, and things will be great.

For example, they may focus only on net profit, and lose sight of the importance of generating an adequate return on investment or positive cash flow. That myopic view can lead to situations where they pursue growth, chase new markets, or seek additional revenue when those things might just be the absolute worst things to do!

Or sometimes, owners focus too much on their businesses' cash flow. They fall into the trap of thinking that if there's cash in their bank, and more of it coming in, then things are rolling right along. That can lead them to situations where they pursue growth opportunities when they really shouldn't. The result is often a devastating cash crunch when the owner is blindsided by something they didn't expect (but should have).

You may have fallen victim to one of those traps in your business. In fact, if you're like most business owners, you probably have. But don't worry. You won't make those mistakes anymore ... at least, you won't after reading this book.

You are going to develop the moneymaking habit for your business (after all, creating the lifestyle you want depends on doing just that). That habit starts with becoming aware that all three of these things must be accomplished in your business, and they must be accomplished at the same time—at least, if your business is going to succeed and make money for you. And it's only by succeeding and making money that your business can serve you, help you build your dream lifestyle, and enable you to achieve whatever other goals you've set for yourself.

TRIPLE OVERLAP—THE KEY TO A MONEYMAKING BUSINESS

A great way to think about the three elements of a money-making business (net profit, return on investment and cash flow) is to picture three different circles. Each of the three elements is treated as a separate circle.

The area where they overlap is the *only place* your business will actually make money for you. Look at the example in Exhibit 2.1.

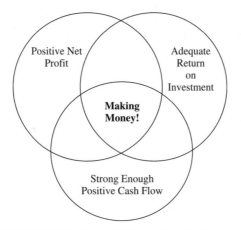

Exhibit 2.1 The Found Money Triple Overlap.

Your goal as a business owner is to constantly pay attention to *all three* elements of making money—positive net profit, adequate return on investment, and positive cash flow—*at all times*. You must manage your business to create a Triple Overlap, and you must make that overlap as large as possible (because that's when it makes you the most money).

WATCH OUT FOR THE DANGER ZONES

The areas inside any one circle, but not in the triple-overlap area, might look appealing. But don't be fooled and get drawn into that trap. They may look appealing, and you might be tempted to focus solely on one of them, but please don't.

Those individual areas outside the Triple Overlap are actually your Danger Zones.

How can they be Danger Zones when they are each part of making money? How can positive net profit be dangerous? Good questions.

In actual fact, each element, itself, isn't dangerous. I call them Danger Zones because they have the potential to lure unsuspecting business owners into a potentially lethal trap. They can take you into areas that can cause very unpleasant consequences. They can seduce the unsuspecting business owner.

You see, an unsuspecting business owner, with some knowledge about one of the three elements, and who focuses on just that one element (the Danger Zone) is going to be fooled into thinking everything is just fine. That owner will end up like the naked emperor in the classic fairy tale, who thought everything was fine when it clearly wasn't.

After all, if a business is making a healthy net profit, it's easy to assume that all is going well. If a business has a strong cash flow, it's easy to assume that things are great. Those assumptions are dead wrong. But it's easy to be seduced if you don't know better.

In the next few chapters, we're going to take a look at each one of those elements. That way, you will have a full understanding of why all three need to happen together for your business to make money.

So take a deep breath. Your life, and your relationship with your business, is about to change. You will never look at your business, your products and services, or your customers the same way again. That's a promise. And I also promise that this is a very good thing.

CHAPTER
3

MAKING MONEY: NET PROFIT

Okay. You now know that your business exists to make money—as much money as it legally, morally, and ethically can. What you do with that money is up to you and will form the basis of your dream lifestyle.

I'm going to assume that you're fine thinking about your business existing to make money for you. If you aren't, do yourself and your loved ones a huge favor. Put this book down, and get out of business now. If you don't believe your business exists to make money, sell it (if you can), close your doors, whatever. Just get out now before you cause any more emotional and financial damage to yourself and your family.

Still here?

Great! As I said, I assume you're okay with your business making lots of money, and with maximizing its profit and cash flow.

Now we're going to look more deeply into a foundational concept of this book and the Found Money system. That fundamental concept is the Triple Overlap (you were introduced to it in Chapter 2, remember?).

This chapter, and the two that follow, are each going to cover one of the elements of the Triple Overlap. This chapter is going to beat up on the Triple Overlap element of Net Profit.

So let's get going.

NET PROFIT

The first of the three elements your business needs to be a money-maker is net profit. This element is probably the one you're most familiar with as a business owner. Most business owners are aware of net profit, because:

- It drives their taxes

- It influences their relationship with their banker

- It's a concept that is understood intuitively

But we're going to cover it in detail.

Now, now. Don't roll your eyes and get bored. This is a great refresher if you "already know it." And it's absolutely critical if you aren't intimately familiar with it.

Even if you think you "know it all," please still pay attention, because you're probably going to find some surprising ways of looking at your net profit—ways you may have never seen before.

WHAT IS NET PROFIT?

Net profit can be defined (my definition, not some stuffy accounting textbook's definition) as the thing that's left over after you gather up all the expenses your business generates and subtract them from all the revenue it creates.

> Net profit is the thing that's left over after you gather up all the expenses your business generates and subtract them from all the revenue it creates.

Do you know what the most important part of that definition is? You've read it twice now. The most important part of that definition for you to *understand* is the words *left over*.

Do you believe it?

I certainly hope so.

You see, an awful lot of business owners "know" the definition of net profit. They *know* that it's the mathematical remainder (and the physical remainder) when all the expenses are subtracted from all the revenues. You probably know it well, too.

But here's the thing. Even though you may know what net profit *is*, you most likely don't *understand* it. At least that's what my years of working with hundreds of business owners have shown me. Some of those businesses were pretty large and sophisticated—and their owners still didn't truly understand net profit.

In fact, to find out whether you truly understand net profit, here's a really brief exercise.

Understanding Net Profit Exercise

Take a look at the financial information depicted in Exhibit 3.1 on page 24, taken from the last three years, for a particular business. Pretend you have just bought the business from its previous owner, and the information below is all you know about it. Then, in the space below the financial data, write down what *you* would do to take control of the net profit trend.

What answers did you come up with?

Of course, you can't really answer me right now (unless you want the person sitting next to you to wonder about your sanity when you start talking to this book—and even then, I couldn't hear you anyway). But I'm willing to go out on a limb here. I have run this little test with business owners many times, and the answers are almost always the same. It doesn't seem to matter what type of business it is, or how much experience the business owner has.

	2006	2007	2008
Sales	$ 100,000	$ 150,000	$ 200,000
Cost of Sales	40,000	82,500	130,000
Overhead	30,000	40,000	50,000
Net Profit	$ 30,000	$ 27,500	$ 20,000

To change the net profit trend, I would:

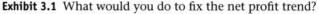

Exhibit 3.1 What would you do to fix the net profit trend?

Because of that, I'm pretty sure your answers will have taken the form of one of the following responses (or some variation of them):

- Increase sales volume

- Reduce cost of sales

- Trim overhead

Now, let me tell you something. Whenever I get answers like those, I instantly know something about the business owner giving those answers. I know that the business owner *knows* the definition of net profit well, yet *understands* it poorly.

Let me explain ...

Hunting for Dinosaurs

The fact that most business owners don't fully understand net profit is demonstrated by their actions. And, as Ralph Waldo

Emerson said, "What you do speaks so loud I cannot hear what you say." It's their actions that truly reveal their lack of understanding—despite what they may say.

Most business owners (and most accountants, too) act as though net profit is something that can be controlled. (In fact, that's what each wrong answer (and their variations) in the previous exercise is trying to do—control net profit.) For example, they create business plans and projections that show that all they need to do is realize a modest increase in sales volume and some reductions in various expenses, and the business will create a much better net profit.

And then they mistakenly assume they've created a plan for improving their net profit. But guess what? It doesn't work that way. In fact, not only is that approach totally ineffective, it's actually very, very dangerous.

You see, the *mathematics* work that way. That's definitely true. If the business creates the projected sales increase and manages to reduce expenses as planned, then net profit will increase as anticipated.

But that approach completely misses the most important part of the net profit definition. Those two little words: *left over*. When you miss the incredible significance of those two tiny words, you miss tapping into the true potential of your business.

Why the heck are those two words so crucial to your business success? Because they focus your attention on the fact that net profit is actually nothing more than a *remnant*—a relic of the past.

It's a dinosaur.

No, it's a fossil. The Merriam-Webster Dictionary defines a fossil as "a remnant, impression, or trace of an organism of past geologic ages ... "[1] And while net profit obviously isn't from an organism, I think you get the point. It's a part of *history*, because net profit can only be calculated and measured *after the fact*.

You see, net profit is nothing more than a summary of the excess (hopefully) of revenues over expenses over a specific time

---

[1]Merriam-Webster Online, www.merriam-webster.com.

period. And because, by definition, it can't be determined until after a certain time period has passed, there's nothing that can be done with it other than to measure it.

In other words, it's simply *impossible* for you to do anything about net profit, other than measure it. Net profit, as a financial concept, is something that just happens. It's like yesterday's high temperature that is always reported on The Weather Network. The high temperature can't be determined until after the fact. It's interesting and useful, in some ways, but there's nothing you can do to change it.

CONTROLLING THE PROCESS OF NET PROFIT

However, you can control the things that *create* net profit. That's because the two components of net profit, revenue and expenses, are created by the activities that go on in your business. It's the performance of those activities that results in revenue and expenses for your business.

In other words, the creation of net profit in your business is a process. The definition of a process is "a series of actions or operations conducing to an end."[2] And that's exactly what net profit is—the culmination of a series of activities.

So there you have it. Creating net profit is nothing more than a process. Because it's a process, you can identify the specific activities and steps in that process that create the end result. And then, just like any other process, if you change (manage) the activities in the process, you alter (manage) the outcome.

The good news for you is that your business isn't really all that complex. It's not a nuclear reactor (unless your business happens to be nuclear reactors!). And that makes it fairly easy to identify, manage, control, and affect the activities that create revenue and expenses in your business. In other words, it's fairly easy to get a handle on, and direct, the *process* of creating net profit.

To drive this point home, here are some examples of things that can affect the process of creating net profit.

---

[2]Merriam-Webster Online, www.merriam-webster.com.

Answering the Phone

The way your team members answer the telephone is one activity in the process of creating net profit. It might seem like a rather mundane activity; it's anything but. Answering the phone is often the first contact a client or prospect has with your business. How that activity is performed has a huge impact on the quantity and quality of customers your business attracts.

If you and your team work to come up with a better, more effective way of answering the telephone, that activity (answering the phone) can create more revenue (when customers buy from you), with no increase in expenses (your wage costs for the team remain the same).

So the activity of answering the phone affects revenue and expenses, which create net profit. But it's only by impacting (altering) the activity that you can actually impact net profit. Remember, net profit is only something that happens after the fact. It's a historical measurement.

A diagram of the activity in this example might look like Exhibit 3.2.

Exhibit 3.2 Example of net profit activities.

Notice how it's the activity of answering the telephone that is the key to creating the revenue and expenses. The activity (answering the phone) is the thing ultimately affecting net profit.

Now imagine, for a moment, the difference between the following two conversations you might have with a new receptionist on his or her first day of work. Think about how clear and how motivating each conversation is, as far as helping the receptionist contribute to the net profit of the business:

1. "We need to increase our net profit. It's your job to play a part in that. I want you to help us make more money."

Or,

2. "The way you answer the phone sets up the entire experience our customers are going to have with us. By responding to *their* questions, and asking specific questions that we've found useful to attract customers, you are one of the engines of our success."

Listening to Your Customers

Listening to your customers is another activity in your business that you control, and that contributes to the creation of net profit.

Your good customers, the ones you love, who love you, and of whom you want more (you'll find out more about this concept and how to address it in Chapter 10, on Customer Profitability Mapping), will tell you all sorts of things that will let you improve your net profit creation process. That is, if you let them. And if you listen to them.

When you create and implement an effective system for talking with and listening to your customers, you will be surprised at what you hear. You will quickly discover which aspects of your business are important to your dream customers. And just as important, you'll learn which aspects really don't matter to them (prepare your ego, these can sometimes sting).

Once you know what matters and what doesn't for your best customers, you've got the potential to create magic in your business.

This activity (listening and responding to your best customers) gives you another way to impact the process your business has for creating net profit. It puts you and your team into the driver's seat.

You can make sure your business has specific actions and a focus on the things that matter to your best customers. Incorporate those things into your systems, so they are done consistently, automatically, all the time. You will be able to do more of the things that are important to your customers, and you'll be able to tell them about it. This approach will give you more control over your pricing and greatly reduce the impact of your competitors.

Your customers will also be much more likely to tell their friends and associates about your business, and create a strong source of referrals for you.

Getting Customers to Come Back More Often

Another activity that can really boost the process of creating net profit is to invite your best customers to come back. It sounds simple, maybe even a little bit silly.

But it doesn't appear to be simple for most businesses. Because even though this activity could be as simple as making a phone call or sending out a specific invitation or letter, it is hardly ever done by most businesses. It just doesn't seem to be an activity most business owners consider.

Here's a story about this very thing. I was talking to a friend of mine a couple of months back about his business and the ways he could increase his net profit (yeah, I talk about and think about these things, even in my spare time).

He told me that his net profit had been pretty much flat over the previous three years. And, he said, he had a hard time knowing whether his advertising was making a difference. He was spending about $25,000 each year on advertising, but his sales just stayed at about the same level (and so did his net profit).

So I asked him how frequently his customers came into his store. At that point he looked through his records, and noted how many of his "good" customers didn't seem to come into the store very often (maybe once a year, or so). He talked about how that puzzled him, because they were good customers, but they just didn't seem to come back very often.

I asked him when he last called or contacted those *specific people* and invited them down to the store. The answer? Never.

He had never thought about specifically inviting these particular customers, with whom he already had a relationship, into the store (or at least, he had never done it). He had never considered inviting them, or telling them about something he thought might interest them, given their previous purchases and tastes. The focus was always on finding another way of advertising in various media to attract new customers into the store.

We agreed to do a test. We planned to mail an invitation to a special evening to the specific "good" customers he had identified. The cost was quite modest—roughly $500 for the postage and printing costs. And it was almost a guarantee that the resulting additional sales would far exceed any new sales that might be generated by spending that same $500 on another "blanket ad."

So what does this mean? That by identifying and contacting specific customers whom he knows, and with whom he has dealt in the past, my friend was going to contact several hundred people who have the following characteristics:

- They know about him and his business.

- He knows about them and likes them.

- He knows they buy and value what he sells.

- He already knows their tastes and preferences.

Compare this to the option of running another radio or print ad that reaches thousands of people, most of whom don't need or want what he sells, and have no experience with him, his business, or his style. Oh yeah, and those radio and print ads would cost considerably more than the $500 he would spend to mail an invitation to his existing customers.

Which one sounds like it makes the most sense?

It's pretty clear that when it's examined in that light, the radio ad is a distant second to the direct approach to existing customers. Therefore, this specific activity (the direct approach) is going to become part of his process of creating net profit.

These are just three simple examples to prime your "mental pump." They are meant to show you how you can manage and control the activities that are part of the process of profit. Remember, you *can't* directly manage and control net profit so stop thinking about it as something you *can* control or manage.

Instead, start thinking of net profit as the logical outcome of a series of activities (a process). You *can* control the activities in the process—and that's how you manage, change, and create the net profit you want from your business.

Later in this book, you will explore ways to identify and improve the activities that create net profit more fully. Now it's time to consider the second element of the Triple Overlap, and in Chapter 4, you're going to do just that.

CHAPTER

4

MAKING MONEY: RETURN ON INVESTMENT

The second element of the Triple Overlap for your business is creating an adequate return on investment (ROI). ROI is actually a simple calculation. What it tells you is how effectively your business uses the money you've got tied up in it to make more money. It is simply a measure of how efficient your business is. Just like an automobile that has a fuel efficiency rating in terms of miles per gallon, ROI measures the profit per dollar for your business.

ROI is actually quite an intuitive concept that we use almost daily in many areas of our lives. For example, financial institutions scream about the rate of interest they will pay us for our deposits. All else being equal, it's only natural that you would deposit your money with the one that's going to give the highest rate of interest (the highest return on your investment). In the same manner, when we consider taking a new job, we weigh the benefits of the new job compared to what we will give up by leaving the old job—and obviously, the more "new benefits" that are gained, compared to the "old benefits" given up, the more attractive the new opportunity.

Clearly, the logic behind measuring ROI is obvious and simple.

But, strangely, when it comes to running a business, this intuitive concept often gets completely ignored (or forgotten) by an awful lot of business owners—and the odds are high that you're one of them. But don't worry. Because from now on, *you* are going to be one of the successful business owners who considers ROI and harnesses its power to create the business you want.

BREAKING IT DOWN

Before we go any further with our discussion about measuring, managing, and controlling ROI, we need to take a look at what return on investment actually means.

"Return" refers to the net profit your business creates. "Investment" refers to the amount of money you've got tied up in the assets (other than cash) of your business.

An asset is something your business owns (compared to a liability, which is something your business owes to someone else). Common examples of assets are cash, accounts receivable, prepaid expenses, inventory, equipment, and other capital assets.

For a more detailed discussion and definition of all the elements of the Found Money system, go to the Web site for this book, at www.foundmoneybook.com. You will find all sorts of cutting edge information, definitions, and free tools there.

The formula used in the Found Money system for ROI is as follows:

$$\text{Return on Investment} = \frac{\text{Net Profit}}{\text{Assets}}$$

ROI measures how much you get out of your business (net profit) compared to how much you put into it (investment in assets). It makes sense, then, that having an ROI that increases over time is a great thing. Business, after all, is all about maximizing resources; the more profit you can get for a given amount of assets, the better it is for you, your business, and your employees.

It also makes sense that, barring some exceptional, specific reason, you *never* want to have ROI decreasing over time. If your ROI decreases, it means you are getting less out of your business, relative to what you've got invested in it, than you used to. And you need to take action quickly.

Sometimes, when it is done intentionally, a temporary decrease in ROI is acceptable. For example, if your business is making a major push into a new market or product line, it's possible that you will be required to invest in higher inventory and other assets to launch into that market. But in these circumstances, it's important to note the decrease in ROI is *only* acceptable if it's been planned for and if there is a concrete plan for quickly bringing it up to acceptable levels again.

EATING SOUP WITH A FORK

A few years ago, while doing some consulting work with a client in Texas, I met the owner of a business who talked about "eating soup with a fork." What this refers to, essentially, is, "being busy just to be busy."

I liked the concept a lot, and the idea really stuck with me. My experience with the business owners I have worked with over the years has convinced me that a failure to pay attention to ROI and to proactively manage it is one of the leading causes of the "eating soup with a fork" syndrome.

Very often, a business that doesn't have an adequate ROI (or has a decreasing ROI over time) causes much of the overwork, stress, and lack of financial success so many business owners experience. The failure to understand, monitor, and control ROI traps many business owners on the endless treadmill of "too much work, not enough pay, and can't afford to hire anyone else."

BACK TO SCHOOL

Think back to when you were learning about fractions in school. It was probably one or two years ago.

Why fractions? Because that's all ROI is—a fraction. To get a really good grasp of the power of ROI, and to effectively harness its energy, you're going to have to use your knowledge about fractions and how they work. You may have told your teacher that you didn't need to learn that stuff, because you'd never use it. Boy, were you wrong.

Lucky for you, your teacher knew you'd need to know it someday and forced you to learn it anyway. You may remember (and if you don't, you will soon) that there are only three ways to make a fraction larger (i.e., to increase your ROI):

1. *Increase the numerator* (the top number); this means growing your net profit

2. *Decrease the denominator* (bottom number in the fraction); this requires you to reduce your investment in assets

3. *Some combination* of the previous two

If you always remember that ROI is just a fraction, and that there are only these three ways to make it larger, you will continually remind yourself to pay attention to both the top and bottom elements.

That may seem obvious right now. But as obvious as it may seem, it is certainly *not* the way most business owners seem to act. It seems most business owners develop a dangerous laser focus on net profit. They fall into the trap of thinking that all they have to do is increase net profit (more sales, cost cutting, or both) and then they will suddenly have all the cash they need and have been seeking for years.

But that's the major reason why they struggle. Too strong a focus on net profit usually leads to the tendency to ignore the business's overall investment in assets. And experience tells each one of us that things that are ignored are not properly managed, in any business.

Failing to properly manage the level of investment in assets almost always leads to a declining ROI, and a business that does not create nearly the amount of money it could for its owners.

That's because there is a natural tendency, in any business, for the investment in assets to grow too quickly, unless it's monitored and actively managed. Managing ROI is hard work. It involves all the things that aren't fun and that business owners tend to want to ignore. It requires making accounts receivable collection calls, setting credit policies and sticking to them, and so on.

But ignoring ROI can be deadly for a business.

Found Money Rule of ROI

Your business cannot make money for you if your investment in assets increases at a faster rate than your net profit.

If this rule is violated, as it so often is, you simply won't see much money from your business—and probably won't see any real money at all!

THE BUSINESS DEATH SPIRAL

Violating the Found Money Rule of ROI will quickly put your business into a Death Spiral—a situation in which your investment in assets starts growing faster than your growth in net profit.

Why can't your business grow its assets at a rate faster than the growth in net profit for an extended period of time? Because it won't be able to generate enough cash to continue its operations. It's going to run out of money. Pure and simple

Of course, as mentioned earlier, it is possible for the investment in assets to temporarily grow faster than net income, and still be acceptable. But only when that situation is intentional and planned—for example, when the business is launching a new product line or division.

But the Found Money Rule of ROI still applies. During a "planned Death Spiral" time period, the business won't make any money for its owners. The business will run out of money during that time period. If the Death Spiral was planned for strategic reasons, hopefully the owners had the foresight to target when that phase would be finished and the business would again start making money. Hopefully, the owners also created a plan to obtain a source of cash to fund the planned Death Spiral.

However, if you allow your business to get into an *unplanned* Death Spiral, it can be disastrous. You must quickly develop a plan and take corrective action to bring the growth in assets back in line with net profit growth. Failing to do that will run your business (and you and your family along with it) smack into a financial wall.

Feed Me

Some of you may recall the movie *Little Shop of Horrors*, about a large man-eating plant with an insatiable appetite. The plant was constantly hungry, demanding "Feeeeed Me!"

That's what your business is like if your investment in assets outstrips your growth in net profit. But when it's your business that's getting ugly and demanding "Feeeeeeed Me" (instead of an animated plant in a movie), it's not cute and charming at all. Instead, it's painful, stressful, emotionally and mentally draining, and financially ruinous.

As long as the Death Spiral is allowed to continue, you will be forced to CONTINUALLY feed cash to your business. It simply won't generate enough cash from operations to continue operating. You'll have to continually feed it more cash, either from your pocket or from banks or other lenders.

Until you stop the Death Spiral and pull your business out of it, not a single dollar of cash is going to flow *out* of your business. If there is no cash that flows out of the business, that means there isn't any extra cash to repay lenders, repay investors, hire more team members, fund growth, or *pay yourself*!

You and your business will be on the classic, yet heartbreaking and soul-destroying, treadmill of being forced to work harder and harder to make less money, and you will be unable to hire more team members to help out. In short, it will be a living hell.

THE DEATH SPIRAL IN ACTION

As David Blaine, street magician extraordinaire, always says in his disclaimers, please *do not* try this at home. We're about to take a look at a fictitious business in a Death Spiral to demonstrate why it's such a dangerous thing, and why it truly hampers your efforts to build a business that serves your dream lifestyle.

Assume that your business is increasing its net profit by a healthy 10% per year. But along with that net profit growth, it has been growing its investment in assets by an annual rate of 12%. To really grasp what's going on here you need to consider that every $1 of additional assets requires an additional $1 of cash.

Notice what's happening in the illustration in Exhibit 4.1. Despite an ever-increasing net profit, this business is continuing to experience a larger and larger cash shortfall each year. Despite achieving record net profit levels each year, more and more cash is required to "Feeeed Me."

Take a moment to consider what is going on in the life of this business owner. Net profit has been increasing by 10% each year.

Year 1	Net Profit	$ 10,000
	Total Assets	$ 100,000
	Return on Investment	10%
Year 2	Net Profit	$ 11,000
	Total Assets	$ 112,000
	Return on Investment	9.8%
	Increase in Assets during Year	$ 12,000
	Net Profit for Year	$ 11,000
	Investment Shortfall	$(1,000)
Year 3	Net Profit	$ 12,100
	Total Assets	$ 125,440
	Return on Investment	9.6%
	Increase in Assets during Year	$ 13,440
	Net Profit for Year	$ 12,100
	Investment Shortfall	$(1,340)
	Total Shortfall	*$ (2,340)*

Exhibit 4.1 A Death Spiral in action.

It's likely that this increase has created much more activity in the business, so it is "busier than it's ever been" each year (ever heard yourself say that?). The owner is no doubt working harder and harder (and longer and longer) to keep up with all that increased activity. But because of the Death Spiral, the owner isn't seeing any reward for the increased effort and sacrifice (there's no cash being created—it's being sucked up instead). And, further, the business doesn't have any excess cash to hire more employees.

If the situation is not stopped, the business owner will end up emotionally and physically drained, probably suffer from relationship problems with family and loved ones, and eventually face financial ruin.

This is a "classic" Death Spiral. You can just feel the plunge into oblivion, can't you?

By the way, the analogy for my Death Spiral comes from aviation. It refers to the dangerous situation (a spiral) when an airplane starts spinning out of control, faster and faster, all the while plummeting toward the ground. If the spiral isn't quickly recognized and stopped, the airplane spirals all the way into the ground at full speed, creating a fiery and deadly crash.

That's how it is when you allow your business to get into a Death Spiral. If you don't realize what's happening fast, and don't take the correct actions quickly, the result is a devastating crash (emotionally, physically, relationship-wise, financially, or all of them).

Growing Out of Business

You may have heard the expression "growing out of business" before.

The term refers to the situation in which a business grows quickly, with a decent gross profit, and the owner thinks he or she has it made. Unfortunately, the growth trajectory of the business combined with a lack of attention to ROI by the owner creates a Death Spiral. Rather than "having it made," the owner is actually hurtling straight toward a fiery crash—and doesn't even realize it.

The business is continually short on cash. The owner can't afford to hire more people and is forced to work harder and harder. But despite working harder and harder, he or she just can't seem to "get ahead" and actually have any cash in the bank.

And paradoxically, in almost every case, the owner incorrectly believes that if he or she could just get more customers, market better, and grow the business even more, the problems would all disappear.

But that's so wrong.

It's very common for the owner of a business in a Death Spiral to make one of the following statements (or some variation, or even all three—I've heard it all!). You may have even said some of the following yourself and didn't realize it for the danger signal it was:

1. "You know, we've never been busier, but there's still no cash in the bank."

2. "I seem to be more in debt now than when I used to be smaller."

3. "I could probably make more money if I shut the business down and went to work for someone else."

Pull Up, Pull Up!

If you ever find your business in a Death Spiral (or if you're in one right now), you must pull out of it.

FAST!

Your business (and you) simply can't continue like that. It's not sustainable, it's not healthy, and it's a huge waste of money, time, and energy. Until you stop the Death Spiral, your business will continue to act as a destructive force in your life. It will take any money, time, and energy that you will give it and almost instantly transform them into a business that's even more bent on self-destruction (and that wants to take you with it!).

It simply isn't sustainable.

If a Death Spiral is not recognized quickly and stopped fast, all your efforts and best intentions won't be enough to prevent a tragic wreck. And along with the death of the business, that wreck will cause a lot of pain and damage to your emotional health and personal finances, too.

Can Marketing Be Dangerous?

When a business is in a Death Spiral, marketing tactics are like a loaded gun. If marketing is not handled with a lot of care, attention, and experience, it can be dangerous. That's because a great marketing effort launched while a business is in a Death Spiral usually results in a bad situation getting even worse.

In a Death Spiral, marketing to the wrong customers, or with the wrong products and services, will just make the existing Death Spiral faster and steeper.

If you've allowed your business to get into a Death Spiral because you haven't properly managed and controlled your ROI, you need to take quick action. You must do some housekeeping before you even think about any type of marketing.

In fact, pairing a dynamite marketing effort that attracts more customers and more growth with a business that doesn't have its financial house in order is just like lighting a match in an old garden shed full of gasoline fumes. It's going to create an explosion that is dangerous and destructive. There's nothing good about it.

DEFEATING THE DEATH SPIRAL

Now let's look at the previous example of the business in a Death Spiral. However, this time we're going to assume the business owner carefully balanced ROI and growth in net profit. What would the results look like in that situation?

Take a look at Exhibit 4.2.

Year 1	Net Profit	$ 10,000
	Total Assets	$ 100,000
	Return on Investment	10%
Year 2	Net Profit	$ 11,000
	Total Assets	$ 110,000
	Return on Investment	10%
	Increase in Assets during Year	$ 10,000
	Net Profit for Year	$ 11,000
	Excess Cash	$ 1,000
Year 3	Net Profit	$ 12,100
	Total Assets	$ 121,000
	Return on Investment	10%
	Increase in Assets during Year	$ 11,000
	Net Profit for Year	$ 12,100
	Excess Cash	$ 1,100
	Total Excess Cash	*$ 2,100*

Exhibit 4.2 The Death Spiral defeated.

The business still realized a growth in net profit of 10% each year (and set record net profits each year). At the same time, the ROI was also kept in balance, and steps were taken to ensure ROI wasn't sacrificed as net profit grew.

At the end of three years, in this example, the business actually created a total of $2,100 in *excess cash* ($1,000 in Year 2 and $1,100 in Year 3). Compare this to the Death Spiral example in Exhibit 4.1, which generated a *cash shortfall* totaling $2,340 over the three years.

By actively managing the business with an eye on *both* net profit and ROI *at the same time*, a cash shortage was converted into a cash surplus. Rather than a deadly Death Spiral, the business owner in the second example created a Power Spiral—an upward trajectory of increasing net profit and excess cash flow. That's definitely what the owner had in mind when she started her business!

The table in Exhibit 4.3 gives a quick summary of the two scenarios.

		Death Spiral	Power Spiral	Difference
Year 1	Net Profit	$ 10,000	$ 10,000	$ 0
	Total Assets	$ 100,000	$ 100,000	$ 0
	Return on Investment	10%	10%	0%
Year 2	Net Profit	$ 11,000	$ 11,000	$ 0
	Total Assets	$ 112,000	$ 110,000	$ (2,000)
	Return on Investment	9.8%	10%	+0.2%
	Increase in Assets during Year	$ 12,000	$ 10,000	$ (2,000)
	Net Profit for Year	$ 11,000	$ 11,000	$ 0
	Excess Cash	$ (1,000)	$ 1,000	$ +2,000
Year 3	Net Profit	$ 12,100	$ 12,100	$ 0
	Total Assets	$ 125,440	$ 121,000	$ (4,440)
	Return on Investment	9.6%	10%	+0.4%
	Increase in Assets during Year	$ 13,440	$ 11,000	$ (2,440)
	Net Profit for Year	$ 12,100	$ 12,100	$ 0
	Excess Cash	$ (1,340)	$ 1,100	$ +2,440
Total Cash Impact for Period		$ (2,340)	$ 2,100	$ 4,440

Exhibit 4.3 The Power Spiral versus the Death Spiral.

Again, it's important to note that the *only* difference between the two scenarios is the ROI. Net profit in both scenarios is exactly the same. ROI was maintained at a consistent 10% in the second one, and was allowed to slide in the first scenario. Yet the difference in this simple example was huge! ROI made the difference between having no cash flow (in fact, having negative cash flow) and having positive cash flow.

ROI is really that important! And its contribution toward creating a money-making business (with a Triple Overlap) is really that powerful.

What Kind of Assets?

Earlier in this chapter, we said that assets were anything that a business owned. Assets can include everything from cash, to accounts receivable, to inventory, to equipment and other capital assets that have been acquired over the years.

Each business is different from the viewpoint of the assets it uses. A manufacturing business will have a large investment (usually) in equipment and machinery and an investment in accounts receivable and inventory. A service business will have a minimal investment in equipment, but it will have a large investment in assets such as accounts receivable and inventory (yes, it does have inventory, as you will see in a few moments).

From the Found Money viewpoint, when it comes to managing a business to maximize its profit, cash flow, and ROI (the Triple Overlap), and avoid or pull out of a Death Spiral, we are primarily concerned with two main assets. The two assets we're most concerned about are inventory and accounts receivable. We're not going to concern ourselves with investments made in fixed assets and other equipment. It's not that those things aren't important; it's just that, when it comes to finding hidden profit and cash flow, accounts receivable and inventory have the most immediate impact. Investments in equipment are longer term and can't be changed nearly as quickly as the investment in accounts receivable and inventory.

This way of looking at ROI differs from traditional accounting and financial views and definitions of ROI. And that's fine. I'm not interested in making you into an accountant or a financial analyst. All I care about is helping you find more money in your business and getting more profit and cash flow out of it. So if your accountant tells you it's "wrong," don't argue. Just smile and know that the way *you* look at it helps you *make money*.

Yes, Your Business *Does* Have Inventory!

Inventory refers to all the assets you've accumulated in your business that you intend to sell to your customers or clients. Inventory is obvious in a retail or manufacturing business, where something is made, or purchased, to be resold.

But what's not so obvious is what I call "hidden inventory." Hidden inventory exists in every business. The reason it's hidden is that traditional accounting does not capture, value, or measure it. And because of that, your accountant doesn't care about it (they're most likely just doing financial statements for reporting and tax purposes, right?). If your accountant doesn't care about it, your banker most likely doesn't either. And that makes it really easy to simply ignore.

But from a Found Money viewpoint, where the goal is to maximize your profit and cash flow, it *does* matter. In fact, it matters a whole lot.

The tendency to ignore hidden inventory, or think your business doesn't have inventory, is actually the fault of financial accounting rules and your accountant. Well, it's not really your accountant's fault—don't blame the accountants, because they certainly aren't trying to hurt you. It's just that they are trained to record historical financial information according to prescribed accounting rules. And those rules are more concerned with reporting to tax and regulatory authorities than with helping you run a better business.

Traditional accounting simply doesn't do a very good job of realizing and tracking hidden inventory. Traditional accounting only looks at inventory as something that has been purchased or manufactured, and is waiting to be resold.

But don't be fooled. For the purpose of managing your business (and making money), you need to consider inventory to be *any* investment you've made into something you expect to sell to a customer. This broader definition of inventory (compared to the accounting definition) explains why many businesses run into problems with the Death Spiral when they don't expect it and certainly don't see a problem coming.

Here's a real life example to illustrate how broad this definition is, and why it matters to you.

When I was forming one of my companies, I hired a young graphic designer who was recommended to me. The guy was sharp, personable, and seemed easy to work with. So here we have a business owner with a graphic design firm. Could he have any inventory issues? Answer that question after I tell you the rest of the story.

He developed a logo, color scheme, cards, and letterhead for me. It was a nice piece of work and I was happy. At one of our meetings, the guy (we'll call him Mike) told me how his business was really exploding. It seems I wasn't the only person who was impressed by his work and his style. His business had grown tremendously in the previous months, and he was starting to feel the stress, Mike told me. That's a normal part of a growing business (or so he thought).

About a month after that first project was done, I called Mike and asked him to do some more work, on another project for me. We met, and he came up with some killer ideas that were fresh, unique, and totally cool. I was excited that this was going to be a great project. We left that meeting with an agreement that some more ideas would be created, and then we'd meet to finalize things in two weeks.

After two weeks, I called Mike to set up our next meeting, and he explained to me that he wasn't ready to meet yet. He'd been overwhelmed with several projects, and wouldn't be able to get me anything for at least another week. He promised to e-mail me some workups the following week, and then we would set up our meeting.

The next week . . . nothing.

Another call revealed that Mike was still swamped and had done some work on my project (maybe half), but was in no position to forward me anything, or set up a meeting.

This scenario continued for about four weeks. I was getting pretty frustrated, but I wanted to give Mike a bit of a break (after all, I liked the guy, and he did produce nice work). And there's something I always like about seeing a new business overcome its obstacles and succeed.

But finally, I was forced to assume I was never going to get my project completed by Mike. I cut my losses, hired another designer, and got my project done.

What does this long story (and no, I'm not whining, there is a purpose) have to do with inventory and managing ROI? Let's look into Mike's business to get an idea of what was happening (or what we can assume was happening).

Recall that Mike got roughly half my project completed. This means he had invested a fair chunk of his time into it. But because of his workload the project could never get completed.

Let's assume Mike's rate was $100 per hour, and that the half-done project had taken 20 hours to get to the halfway point. That means Mike had, essentially, $2,000 of revenue that was built up waiting to be "sold" (can't sell it until the work is actually done).

Now clearly, Mike didn't have that actual amount invested in the project. Let's say his time would be worth $50 an hour if he worked as an employee for someone else. That means my half-done project would have an actual investment of $1,000 (the opportunity cost of that time if it had been worked for someone else) stuck in Mike's business as inventory. It is money Mike has invested (an opportunity cost), waiting to sell it to a customer (me).

Now, I knew from discussions I had with Mike that he had several clients at that time. And based on my experience, I think it's a safe assumption that I wasn't the only client experiencing delays. Mike's business grew very quickly, and he was caught in the trap of working a little bit on everyone's project to try to keep as many clients as possible partially satisfied that their work was progressing.

If we assume that Mike had 30 clients at that time (I have no clue whether that's the real number, but we'll assume it is for argument's sake), and they were all the same as me, he would have a total inventory (hidden inventory) of $30,000 (30 clients × $1,000).

That would be his investment in inventory—his investment in half-completed projects that were stuck in limbo.

And that $30,000 is *truly* inventory, even though it's not traditionally thought of that way. From a business profitability and money-making point of view, though, it is inventory. It represents an asset that Mike invested in (by putting his time and talent into the projects) that he was expecting (hoping?) to eventually sell to his customers. But because of his rapid growth and delays, that investment continued to grow, without being quickly and effectively converted into cash. That caused the investment in assets to grow at a faster rate than the growth in his net profit.

Mike had allowed his inventory to get out of control. And along with that loss of control, he lost control of his ROI. That means Mike's business is in a Death Spiral. It's growing quickly, and its net profit is growing too. But because he hasn't properly managed his return on investment, he has gotten into the classic situation of being busy, but unable to hire anyone to help him.

He has allowed his ROI to go into the tank!

As long as Mike allows his business to remain in its Death Spiral, Mike and his business are going to be stuck being really busy, fighting fires, struggling to keep up, and still being short on cash (i.e. being unable to hire an employee to help him out).

If Mike continues in this manner, his business will not be sustainable. I hope he realizes it and takes some quick steps to fix the problem, before it's too late for him and his business. (But I don't think so. While I was finalizing this book, several months after the stalled project, Mike called me to say he had some time and could restart my project. Curious, I called Mike back and left a voicemail message saying I'd like to meet with him and talk about a new project I might have. It's been more than a week now, and he still hasn't gotten around to calling me back).

Accounts Receivable—A Customer Is Someone Who Actually Pays!

Your investment in Accounts Receivable (A/R) is the other major area that concerns us in the Found Money system. Accounts receivables are the amounts your customers owe you for products or services they have already purchased and you have already provided to them.

When your business has accounts receivable, you have essentially extended credit to those customers. This is a big thing for the success of your business. It represents cash that you've locked into your business until it's collected.

Not every business has accounts receivables. Some businesses don't have any. They collect payments for their products and services at the time the sale is made. Many retail stores operate this way. Restaurants and gas stations are other examples.

A lot of businesses, however, are in industries where the convention is for customers to pay some time after the products or services are purchased. A common example is the construction industry. Almost every single business involved with this industry provides its products and services and then is paid for them after the fact—sometimes, long after the fact.

In businesses that have accounts receivable, several key things can help manage ROI and help keep it in line with the rate of net profit growth (thus avoiding a Death Spiral). These things are all very simple, but so many businesses don't do them. And that's most likely because, while these things are simple to do, so many business owners just don't understand how important it is to manage ROI and how to do it.

But you're a different breed of business owner. You're a business owner who is developing the understanding and knowledge to actually build a business that makes you money.

Two simple (but critical) ways to help manage your Accounts Receivable (and, therefore, ROI) include:

- Setting payment terms for your customers before you make the sale or provide the service

- Asking all new customers for at least one or two credit references (not necessarily the formal credit bureaus, but just some other businesses in your area with whom they have dealt, so you can ask about their repayment track record)

- Setting limits for the total outstanding accounts receivable any particular customer is allowed to have with your business. These are traditionally called credit limits and are the maximum amount any customer can owe to you at any particular time. If the customer goes over this limit, no more sales will be made to that customer until he or she brings the total back under their limit.

You have now developed an understanding of two out of the three elements of the Triple Overlap. In Chapter 5, you will learn about the third element. So keep going . . .

CHAPTER
5

MAKING MONEY: POSITIVE CASH FLOW

Cash to your business is like oxygen to your blood. Oxygen provides you with the life-sustaining nutrients your body needs to live. And cash gives your business its ability to thrive and function. Your body can't last long without oxygen, and your business can't last long without cash.

Cash flow refers to the way cash comes into your business, the way it flows out of your business, and how much of it ends up sticking around (a good thing). It can sometimes be a little tough to grasp, but it's important to understand, because it reveals an awful lot about what's "going on under the hood" in your business.

WHAT IS CASH FLOW?

Cash flow is simply *all* the cash that comes *into* your business, less *all* the cash that flows *out of* your business. Think of cash as the ocean tide. It sweeps into your business, and then sweeps out again. It ebbs and flows in a continual, endless cycle.

And while it ebbs and flows, you must use your good business skills and management to ensure that not all of the cash that sweeps into your business sweeps back out. You need to make sure that some (more is always better) cash stays behind with each cycle.

Common sources of cash inflows in your business are:

- Cash sales

- Collecting accounts receivable

- Cash from borrowing

- Cash investors have injected into your business

- Cash from selling a piece of equipment or other assets

- Cash invested by owners (good old you)

Common sources of cash outflows are:

- The payment of wages and other operating expenses

- Repayments made on loans

- Payments to shareholders and owners

- Paying accounts payable

- Purchasing new equipment or other assets

WHAT CASH FLOW IS NOT

It is critical that you are totally clear about something. Please pay attention, because this trips up a lot of business owners. You must understand:

CASH FLOW IS NOT NET PROFIT!

Do you recall, in Chapter 3, we discussed how net profit is simply the mathematical remainder—the amount left when all the expenses of your business are subtracted from all your revenues? Hopefully you do. If not, take a few minutes and read Chapter 3 again.

You will notice that nowhere in that definition of net profit is there a single reference to cash. Go ahead and read it again. See? No mention about cash in the definition of net profit.

So what? It means that it's entirely possible to have a business with a strong net profit, but very poor (or even negative) cash flow. It's also possible to have a business with really strong cash flow and low net profit (or even a net loss).

How is that possible? I'm not going to tell you. Just joking! Of course I'll tell you. That's the entire purpose of this chapter, right?

To see how that is possible, look back at the Death Spiral example in Chapter 4. Net profit was positive and growing each year, yet cash flow was actually negative! The Death Spiral caused all the additional cash created, *plus more*, to be tied up in more and more assets each year.

Cash flow is a critical element of the Triple Overlap needed for your business to make money. Cash flow is what actually gives *you* the resources to expand your business and hire more team members, so you can pursue other interests and live your life at a higher level.

Cash flow makes it possible for your business to function. It's a simple fact that you can't "spend" net profits or assets. All you can spend is cash. If you don't believe that, next time you're trying to buy a candy bar, simply bring out your financial statements and tell the clerk that your business made money, and you'll give them $1 of that net profit for the candy bar, then walk out. See how far you get before the police arrive and grab you for shoplifting. (Don't really try this, naturally, but I think you get my point).

YOUR GROWTH LIMITER

It's a frequent occurrence (in fact, it happens so frequently that it's practically a "law") for a business that is growing rapidly to experience very tight cash flow (in fact, it's usually negative). If you think back to Chapter 4, on ROI, you should now understand why this is true.

A business that is growing will generally be increasing its investment in assets. Increased growth almost always requires increased levels of inventory and accounts receivable. Of course, the growth in inventory and accounts receivable should be minimized by using marketing tactics that aim only at the right customers and by promoting the right products and services. And very often, additional investments in equipment and other assets are required for a growing business. All these increases in assets suck up cash quickly.

The natural tendency of business owners to focus on sales growth (almost always the top priority, it seems) rather than net profit (which is what really matters, but surprisingly it is often given much less attention than sales growth) means that usually, accounts receivable and inventory are not carefully monitored. And that allows large increases in accounts receivable and inventory (along with their drain on cash flow) to sneak up on the unsuspecting business owner—a situation that leads to unnecessarily tight (negative) cash flow for the business and needless pain and stress for the owner.

Of course, you won't fall into that trap any longer. You know better. Right?

Owning and running a moneymaking business requires you to maintain the balancing act between net profit, return on investment, and cash flow. You must continually keep an eye on *all* these things and always monitor *all three* of them. Your goal must be to keep them *all* in *balance*.

> Your business can never grow faster than your cash flow allows.

When I ran my own accounting practice, I could immediately tell when a business owner didn't understand this law of business. When we had finished going over the person's income statement, and they saw the bottom-line net profit they had generated, they would say something like this:

"How can you say I made that much money? There's nothing in my bank account!"

This comment, or some variation of it, has been heard by *every* accountant who has ever gone over a set of financial statements with a client. It's probably been uttered by almost every business owner at some time in his or her life, too.

To help you understand cash flow, and how to manage it, Exhibit 5.1 contains a little formula for calculating the cash flow for your business.

	Net Profit from Business
+	Accounts Receivable at *start*
−	Accounts Receivable at *end*
+	Inventory at *start*
−	Inventory at *end*
+	Accounts Payable at *end*
−	Accounts Payable at *start*
+	Cash from assets *sold*
−	Cash paid to *purchase* new assets
+	Depreciation/amortization
−	Debt at *start*
+	Debt at *end*
	Cash Flow!

Exhibit 5.1 Calculating cash flow from your business.

A close look at this formula shows why it's possible for your business to earn a nice, tidy net profit and still be starved for cash. You see, net profit is only the *starting point* for cash flow. There's an awful lot of things that happen to net profit as it travels through the formula and turns into cash flow. There *is* a relationship between cash flow and net profit, but it's an indirect connection.

And it's the fact that they are two different things that requires you to pay attention to cash flow as well as net profit. Not paying attention to the cash flow formula, by the way, is a very common habit (a bad habit) for legions of business owners. It's usually caused by a failure to realize what exactly controls cash flow (the elements of this formula).

And actually, it's usually a very fixable problem. In most cases, poor, or negative, cash flow can be stopped and the situation can be improved easily and quickly. The owner usually ended up in this situation because he or she wasn't paying attention to a few key things. It can most often be turned around quickly by taking some simple corrective actions.

How simple?

Here's an example I came across while working with a client a few years back that demonstrates just how simple it can be. The client was in the aviation business. The company had a high net profit, but almost always seemed to be struggling for cash flow.

During one of our meetings, while mapping out some of the operational flows, two big issues became obvious:

1. The business wasn't sending out monthly statements of account to its customers. Only a copy of the original invoice was sent to each customer. What ended up happening was that a customer's accounting department would lose or misfile an invoice. Since there were no subsequent monthly statements sent, the customers got no further indication that they had missed recording a payable and owed money to my client.

   Eventually, the client would call the customer about an outstanding invoice, but only after it hadn't been paid for two or three months. The mistake in the customer's accounting department would be uncovered then, and the customer would request a copy of the unpaid invoice, which would then be entered into their payable system. Finally, about two months after this duplicate invoice was sent, the business would finally receive payment on that invoice.

   That cash flow lag could have easily be shortened simply by sending out monthly statements in addition to the actual invoices.

2. The business was sending out its invoices at the end of each week.

   The problem with that practice was that a single invoice would typically be for several thousand dollars. Waiting until the end of each week meant that at times, tens of thousands of dollars would sit until the start of a new month (depending on when the actual end of any particular month happened to fall in a week).

That lag meant that the earliest those invoices would be received and processed by corporate clients could be almost two months after the flights were flown.

By changing to a policy of immediately sending out an invoice once a flight was completed, the collection of accounts receivable would begin to improve. And that, naturally, would help improve cash flow.

So there you have a classic example of two very simple activities that a business was able to change, both of which had a large positive impact on cash flow. In almost every instance where a business is suffering from poor (or even negative) cash flow, it really can be just that simple to get it turned around.

To help you really understand the difference, and the link, between cash flow and net profit, let's move on to look at an example. Exhibit 5.2 contains some financial information for a fictitious business. Susan, the owner, has come to you for help. She is distraught. Her business has blossomed and has become one of the most popular of its kind in her town. She was even forced to purchase an additional $20,000 of equipment to keep up.

Susan tells you that she is working almost constantly to keep up with the workload. Her business has never been better, yet, she says, she never seems to have any cash in her bank account. She tells you that she can't keep going like this, but can't afford to hire anyone. She looks at you and asks for help.

	Year 1	Year 2
Net Profit	$ 30,000	$ 40,000
Accounts Receivable	5,000	25,000
Inventory	10,000	20,000
Accounts Payable	7,500	9,000
Loans	12,000	15,000
Depreciation	2,500	5,000

Exhibit 5.2 Susan's business information.

On the face of it, it might look like Susan's business is doing great. Net profit has increased by 33%! That's an absolutely staggering pace of growth. Traditional thinking would say that Susan's got a great thing going. But let's calculate her cash flow to see if she's actually generating any cash and putting some of that increased activity into her bank account.

Let's use the cash flow formula in Exhibit 5.3 to convert her net profit into cash flow and then compare the two.

		Cash Flow Effect
	Net Profit from Susan's Business	**$ 40,000**
+	Accounts Receivable at *start*	5,000
−	Ending Accounts Receivable at *end*	(25,000)
+	Inventory at *start*	10,000
−	Inventory at *end*	(20,000)
+	Accounts Payable at *end*	9,000
−	Accounts Payable at *start*	(7,500)
−	Equipment Purchased	(20,000)
+	Depreciation	5,000
+	Debt at *end*	15,000
−	Debt at *start*	(12,000)
	Cash Flow	**$ (500)**

Exhibit 5.3 Calculating Susan's cash flow.

It's clear that despite Susan's high growth in net profit, her cash flow has remained almost flat (actually, slightly negative). And that's one of the causes of the trap she's currently in. She has found herself in the sad, unnecessary, yet all-too-common situation of wanting (needing) to hire additional team members to keep up with the increased growth and activity, but simply being unable to "afford" it.

Her pain becomes even more apparent when you realize that for her net profit to have grown 33%, her overall sales volume and activity would have exploded by an even larger amount. But her negative cash flow means that despite the massive increase in activity, she can't hire any more team members to help her cope with the increased workload.

At least, she can't hire anyone to help her unless she invests more of her own money, or gets additional debt. She's got herself trapped.

You may have noticed that the word "afford" was in quotes. And that's because Susan probably *can* afford to hire someone to help her out. But to do that, she needs to become a better manager of her cash flow. If she does that, a lot more cash will flow into her bank account, and she will be able to hire more team members to help her.

The truth is that when your business is not creating a strong, positive cash flow, you become a slave to it. You are forced to work your heart and soul out just to keep your business afloat. As long as you allow cash flow to remain weak and you don't actively monitor and manage it, there's simply no way for you to effectively grow your business, reduce your workload, and improve your lifestyle.

It's like living a nightmare.

But now you can wake up, and banish that bad dream forever. Because now you understand cash flow more clearly.

Now that you are familiar with the concept of the Triple Overlap, and the three elements that create it, you can move on to Chapter 6, where you will answer a very critical question …

CHAPTER

6

Is *Your* Business Making You Money?

Thank you.

For what, you ask?

For plowing through the previous chapters. They might have felt pretty tough some of the time (or all of the time, you can tell me the truth, I can take it—not really, humor me at least). But you've now created a solid foundation of understanding so that you can create a business that serves your dream lifestyle by creating enough money. And with that foundation, you have become a member of a very elite group. You are now part of the very small group of business owners in the world who truly understand how their business actually makes money.

You understand what the Triple Overlap is, what it means, and why it's so important. You know each of the three elements that combine to create your Triple Overlap, and how they must occur at the same time for your business to make you money.

And that means you can start working on creating (or recreating) your business to serve your dream lifestyle. You can start finding all the profit and cash flow that's hiding right there, in your business, right now.

With this solid foundation, you can dig deeper into the inner workings of your business. And you can get to the really fun stuff—working on the details and activities that will produce *exactly* the kind of business you want to have. A business that, up until now perhaps, you've only dreamed about.

WHERE ARE YOU NOW?

Have you ever tried to find a specific location and had to call someone for directions? Admit it. We've all been there a time or two before. When you call the other person for directions, what's the first thing they ask you before giving you a single direction?

"Where are you right now?" or something similar is the first question they ask. That question makes total sense. After all, if the other person isn't clear where you're starting, their best intentions and most skillful directions will be entirely useless to you. It's not until they understand your starting point that they can help direct you to where you want to go.

And your business is no different.

You're going to be working hard to take your business somewhere new. Somewhere where it's in tune with your dream lifestyle, where it becomes a vehicle for you to create the life you want.

But before you can decide what you need to do to get there, you first have to figure out exactly where your business is *right now*. You must discover where your business is in terms of your Triple Overlap (or whether you even have a Triple Overlap).

Don't get worried or concerned. The simple fact is that it doesn't matter where your business is right now. You can take control of it and start moving it where you want it to go. What does matter, however, is that you know where you are starting from. Once you know that, you can create a roadmap to take you and your business wherever you want it to be.

There is very little reading to be done is this chapter. This is a working chapter. It's going to help you get an exact picture of where your business is right now, and how well it's been doing at creating a Triple Overlap.

IS YOUR BUSINESS MAKING MONEY?

It's time for you to take a hard look at your own business. You are going to examine the three most recent fiscal years your business has completed. If you prefer, or if it makes more sense for your business, you can choose the three most recent periods other than fiscal years. For example, you might decide to use the three most recent quarters, if your business is in its first year.

Fill in the information from your financial statements in the places indicated in the worksheets provided. Please do these exercises, as well as the other exercises in this book. Don't cheat yourself out of improving your business and your life. Make a real effort, take the time, and complete the exercises. Don't leave any more profit and cash flow hiding in your business.

But be forewarned. You will probably find that it will take a little work on your part.

In fact, when I do my consulting work with individual business owners, an awful lot of them actually don't know where their previous three years' financial statements are. They have never seen the value in them before (other than for tax compliance and something to give their banker). In a lot of cases, they need to phone their accountant and ask for additional copies, because they can't find theirs!

But it really doesn't matter what you have to do. Gather up your financial statements and do this exercise. It's going to give you an honest view of where your business is going, how well it's been doing at making you money, and what kind of potential has been slipping right through your fingers.

You may have to go back to the previous chapters to refresh yourself on how to do some of the calculations. And that's fine. This book is meant to be used, and to be a reference tool you can keep coming back to again and again. The exercise is shown as Exhibit 6.1.

Next, we have a cash flow worksheet in Exhibit 6.2 to help you calculate your cash flow for each year. It looks a little more complicated, but don't let that panic you. Just follow along and let the worksheet guide you through the process.

Summary of "Triple Overlap" For _____

		Most Recent Year	Percentage Change	Next Most Recent	Percentage Change	Next Most Recent
A	Net Profit					
B	Total Assets					
A/B × 100	ROI					
From Cash Flow Worksheet	Cash Flow					

The Cash Flow worksheet is found in Exhibit 6.2. Use it as your template to calculate the Cash Flow for your business.

Exhibit 6.1 Your Triple Overlap worksheet.

	Most Recent Year	Next Most Recent Year	Next Most Recent Year
Net Earnings			
Add	+	+	+
A/R at start			
Subtract	–	–	–
A/R at end			
Add	+	+	+
Inventory at start			
Subtract	–	–	–
Inventory at end			
Add	+	+	+
A/P at end			
Subtract	–	–	–
A/P at start			
Add	+	+	+
Cash from equipment sold			
Subtract	–	–	–
Cash to buy new equipment			
Add	+	+	+
Depreciation			
Add	+	+	+
Debt at end			
Subtract	–	–	–
Debt at start			
Cash Flow			

Exhibit 6.2 Your Cash Flow calculation worksheet.

CHAPTER

7

WHICH PRODUCTS MAKE YOU MONEY?
(And Which Ones Don't?)

Hold onto your motivation for this chapter. We're going to cover some very important things that will set you free—free to find every dollar of profit and cash flow that is waiting to be discovered in your business. Free to understand key distinctions and to be able to make decisions that help your business make money for you. You will learn how to be in control of the financial results your business creates.

You're about to see how the concept of the Triple Overlap can be applied to your *products and services*. You'll learn how it can be used to determine how much money each product and service your business sells actually makes for you. Some of the terms will change slightly in this chapter, but the Triple Overlap concepts still apply.

A foundational element of this chapter, and in analyzing the product Triple Overlap, is Gross Margin. Gross Margin is an awesome and powerful tool to help any business succeed and thrive. If you're like most business owners, you will find this concept truly mind-expanding.

Now, I'll admit parts of the following discussion may be a little bit dry. I have tried my absolute best to make them as "un-dry" as possible, so it shouldn't be too bad. But I still wanted to give you a little warning, because even if you find the next little bit somewhat dry, it is still ultra-important and will form the foundation for a lot of the good stuff that follows. Getting a solid understanding of the information in this chapter will put you in the best position to get control of the financial results your business produces, and you will be able to *create* the financial results you desire for your dream lifestyle.

Let's start by taking a look at the concept of Gross Margin and why it is so important.

GROSS MARGIN—IT'S CRITICAL!

Gross Margin is the most important element of any business, yet paradoxically, it is the least understood by most business owners. Why is it so important? Because understanding and using Gross Margin in your business can do any of the following:

- Identify the products or services you should sell more of

- Identify the products or services you should, or must, sell less of

- Help you decide how to sell your products and services

- Identify the customers (and the types of customers) that actually make your business money

- Identify the customers (or types of customers) that are a drain on your profit, fun, and free time

- Protect you from poor market conditions

- Enable you to avoid fear and confidently take action in situations where your competitors struggle (it can even allow you to expand profitably when others shrink or cower in fear)

- Help you develop strategies, tactics, and actions that will enable you to move your business to a point where it provides you with your dream lifestyle

- Help you find profit and cash flow that's currently trapped and hidden in your business

The concept of Gross Margin and its application ripples through almost *everything* that happens in your business. And because of that, Gross Margin is also a foundational element in the Found Money system, its tools, and its processes.

A SURPRISE FOR ME

I'm always surprised (even though it's happened so many times that I really shouldn't be any more) by just how many business owners don't really understand Gross Margin. I'm not just talking about new businesses or really small businesses, either. I include people who have been in business for many years and have some pretty large businesses.

There simply isn't a strong understanding of Gross Margin, nor an appreciation for its power, what it means, and why it matters. And because of that, an awful lot of business owners miss out on an awful lot of opportunities to maximize their profit, cash flow, and fun.

Even worse than missing those opportunities is that those owners end up living in fear. When a business owner doesn't understand Gross Margin, that owner isn't truly in control of the business and the money it makes. The owners feel that they aren't in control (and they're right), so they live in constant fear that their business won't be profitable, or that it will be damaged or even be destroyed by market conditions, competitors, or a sagging economy.

But that's not the way it has to be at all. A solid grasp of Gross Margin can show any business owner the path to take to *create* the financial results they want and maximize their profit and cash flow. In a good economic environment or a bad one, in the face of heavy competition or no competition, an understanding of Gross Margin shows any business owner which products and services they should sell, and even how to go about selling them.

A solid understanding of Gross Margin can help any business owner survive and succeed in any economic or competitive environment.

Why is a concept that is so important, and so vital to a successful business and economy, so poorly understood? I believe there are two big reasons for this puzzling phenomenon.

The first reason is that many business owners turn to their accountants to help them understand the "financial end" of their business. That's a natural thing for a business owner to do, as their accountant is the one most expert in preparing their financial statements, tax compliance requirements, and tax planning. But the problem with that assumption is that the vast majority of accountants don't really understand the true power of Gross Margin, either.

Oh sure, they can calculate it, define it, and identify it. But that's just the "theory" part of it. It pretty much seems to end there for most accountants. What most (I'd say all, but I don't want to generalize, so I won't) accountants don't seem to have learned is how to actually *use* Gross Margin to improve a business and *create* financial results in the future.

But let's not dogpile on the accountants too much (after all, I am one, and I used to run my own firm before creating the Found Money system and my consulting firm). After all, your accountant is primarily focused on ensuring your business presents accurate *historical* financial statements and complies with tax regulatory requirements. And frankly, that leaves them with little time to do much else.

In addition to not having the time, most accountants simply don't have the training (or the mindset) to dissect Gross Margin and help business owners truly harness its power. Most programs that lead to certification as an accountant focus on training accountants to be able to accurately report historical financial results according to prescribed accounting rules and regulations. Minimal attention is given to Gross Margin and its related issues.

The second reason that Gross Margin is largely misunderstood is that it looks a little bit scary at first. It looks like a bunch of "dry, boring accounting stuff." And because of that, a lot of business owners don't really try to understand it; they assume that it's "just some accounting thing."

But that's judging a book by its cover. And your mother always told you not to do that, remember? So don't do it. After all, she also told you to always wear clean underwear, and you listened to her on that one. (You did, didn't you?)

THE UGLY DUCKLING OF A SUCCESSFUL BUSINESS

Because Gross Margin tends to be ignored by a lot of accountants and most business owners, it is like the "Ugly Duckling" we all remember from childhood fairy tales. It starts out looking ungainly and unpleasant. But given the chance and enough time, this Ugly Duckling will blossom into a beautiful swan. And not just any swan, but one that makes you money. How great is that? (Maybe that makes this Ugly Duckling a Golden Goose!)

So consider yourself warned. This next section may seem a little bit boring and dry, like a typical accounting book. But suck it up and stick with it! I promise you, this isn't an accounting book. And I will only give you the stuff you really need to know so you can acquire the power to create the financial results you want and maximize the profit and cash flow your business produces. Even if it seems boring to you, trust me, it's important that you stay with me.

Two Things

Your business must do two things to help create the financial results you want and maximize your profit and cash flow. Those things are:

1. Offer a product or service that people want

2. Sell them to people who are willing and able to pay for them

That may seem obvious. And it is obvious. But what always shocks me is that, despite being obvious, it doesn't stop a lot of business owners from acting as though those two things simply don't exist. For example, I so often hear business owners say things like "I know I really should pay more attention to this stuff, but ... " Comments like those drive me nuts! They indicate that although the solution is obvious, the person making those comments is still failing to do anything to proactively create any future.

And frankly, that's a loser's attitude. You're *not* a loser, so please don't act like one!

To accomplish those two things, you must fully understand Gross Margin, because you will want to make sure your business is selling the *most profitable products* to the *most profitable customers*.

> You maximize the profit your business gives you *only* when you sell the most profitable products and services to the most profitable customers.

Think about that for a moment. If you could only sell 100 "things" in any given year, wouldn't it make sense to sell the 100 that made you the most money?

Of course it would.

And to find out which 100 things made *you* the most money, you need to understand and use Gross Margin. Once you understand and use Gross Margin, you will discover it can do *all* of the following things:

- It can completely change your relationship with your business and lead you toward your dream lifestyle goals.

- It can give you the perspective you need to get the absolute maximum results from every single element of your business.

- It points, like a laser beam, to the exact products, customers, and services that create the most profit for your business.

- It lets you create marketing strategies and tactics to attract and retain the most profitable customers.

- It streamlines your efforts and those of your team by showing what you can *stop* doing (thus freeing up a ton of time for you and your employees to do other, more profitable stuff).

GROSS MARGIN—WHAT IS IT?

While the concept of Gross Margin and what it can do is amazingly powerful, Gross Margin, itself, is nothing more than a simple calculation. Its power comes from understanding what it means and how it can be used.

Gross margin is simply the difference between the amount you sell a product or service for, and the direct costs of that product or service. Direct costs are the costs that only occur when you buy, sell, create, and provide your products and services. For example, the cost of items purchased from a supplier for resale is a direct cost. The total of all the direct costs for a particular product or service is called the Cost of Goods Sold (COGS) for that particular product or service.

The fact that COGS is made up of a bunch of direct costs, and those costs only occur when a product or service is created and sold, means that COGS goes up and down in proportion to the level of sales volume of any product or service. In other words, COGS varies in direct proportion to your sales volume. For example, assume you sell a product that has a COGS of $100. If you sell five more units, your Cost of Goods Sold will increase by $500 (5 units × $100 COGS per unit).

Now, back to Gross Margin. It is calculated using the following formula:

Gross Margin = Sales Price – Cost of Goods

Exhibit 7.1 includes a simple example to demonstrate.

Sales Price	$200
Cost of Sales	120
Gross Margin	$ 80

$$\text{Cost of Sales (\%)} \quad = \quad \frac{120}{200} = 100$$

$$= \quad 60\%$$

$$\text{Gross Margin (\%)} \quad = \quad \frac{80}{200} = 100$$

$$40\%$$

Exhibit 7.1 Gross Margin calculation.

GROSS MARGIN VERSUS GROSS PROFIT

Gross Margin and Gross Profit are often used interchangeably to refer to the same thing. I don't treat them as the same thing, and the Found Money system doesn't either. They are related, but are definitely two different things.

Gross Margin is the sales price of a product or service less its Cost Of Goods Sold (the formula and discussion you just finished reading). In other words, by definition, it is something that is computed for *each product or service*.

Gross Profit, on the other hand, is the *total* of the Gross Margins for each product and service your business sells, multiplied by the quantity of each product and service that is sold. In other words, Gross Profit is a "summary number" that contains information from several different Gross Margin numbers. Unless, that is, your business only has one product or service. If that's the case, shame, shame on you. But don't get me started. All in due time.

For example, consider a business that has the financial information shown in Exhibit 7.2.

Item	Sales Price ($)	Cost ($)	Gross Margin (%)	Units Sold
A	15	11	$4 (26.7%)	12,000
B	8	4	$4 (50.0%)	30,000
C	19	15	$4 (21.1%)	16,667

Exhibit 7.2 Product Gross Margin information.

The Gross Margin for each different item the business sells is shown in the table. Gross Profit for this business would then be calculated as shown in Exhibit 7.3.

Item A	$4 × 12,000	=	$ 48,000
Item B	$4 × 30,000	=	$ 120,000
Item C	$4 × 16,667	=	$ 66,668
Gross Profit			$ 234,668

Exhibit 7.3 Gross Profit calculation.

This emphasis on treating Gross Margin and Gross Profit as two different things is not just some freakish wordplay. I'll admit, I may be a bit of a geek but I like to think I'm at least a cool geek. The difference between Gross Margin and Gross Profit is a critical distinction in the Found Money system.

It's important because it's actually Gross Profit that counts. Why? Because to maximize the profit, fun and free time you get from your business, and to make it serve your dream lifestyle, you must maximize Gross Profit. It is Gross Profit that enables your business to pay your overhead; to pay wages to your talented team (top wages, right?); to pay yourself; and to continue to grow, thrive, and be safe from economic conditions beyond your control.

The bigger you can make your Gross Profit, the more flexibility you will have to live your dream lifestyle, take advantage of new opportunities, and weather economic storms.

When it comes to Gross Profit, size really does matter.

And to make your Gross Profit as large as possible, given your business, its products and services, and its customers, you need to go through a process called Gross Margin Analysis. And that's just what we're going to cover next.

GROSS MARGIN ANALYSIS

Gross Margin Analysis is the process of analyzing your products and services to determine which are the most profitable. Which ones make your business the most money? Which ones make the least money? Which ones actually lose your business money?

The result of a Gross Margin Analysis is a crystal-clear picture of where to focus your efforts so that your business will create the most money for you, with the least amount of effort.

The best way to see how Gross Margin Analysis works is to look at an example. Assume your business has the data shown in Exhibit 7.4.

Item	Sales Price ($)	Cost ($)	Annual Sales ($)	Average Inventory ($)	Average A/R ($)
A	15	11	180,000	26,250	18,000
B	8	4	240,000	113,000	85,000
C	19	15	317,000	30,000	100,000

Exhibit 7.4 Gross Margin Analysis sample data.

Exhibit 7.5 displays some financial facts for this particular business, given the data provided. Please note that some parts of the following table may not be clear to you at this point. That's okay; they will become clear as you go through the next several sections in this chapter.

		Product A	Product B	Product C
(A) Sales ($)		$180,000	$240,000	$317,000
(B) Sales (% of Total)		24%	33%	43%
(C) Gross Margin (%)		27%	50%	21%
(D) Gross Margin ($)	= A × C	$48,600	$120,000	$66,570
(E) Gross Margin (% of Total)		21%	51%	28%
(F) Average Price per Unit		$15	$8	$19
(G) Number Sold		12,000	30,000	16,684
(H) Gross Margin ($) per Item	= F × C	$4	$4	$4
(I) Avg. Inventory		$26,250	$113,000	$30,000
(J) Avg. Inventory (% of Total)		16%	67%	18%
(K) Inventory Turnover	= I * 365 / (A − D)	73 days	344 days	44 days
(L) Average A/R		$18,000	$85,000	$100,000
(M) Average A/R (% of Total)		9%	42%	49%
(N) A/R Turnover	= (L / A) * 365	37 days	129 days	115 days
(O) ROI	D / (I + L)	110%	61%	51%

Exhibit 7.5 Gross Margin Analysis results.

What does the Gross Margin Analysis tell us? There are several things that quickly jump out.

1. Product C is the product that creates the largest total sales volume ($317,000, or 43% of total sales revenue). Despite representing such a large proportion of total sales revenue, however, its Gross Profit ($66,570) is only 28% of the total Gross Profit for the business. That's because, while the business might sell a lot of Product C, its Gross Margin is relatively low (only 21%). In other words, for every $100 of Product C sold, only $21 is available as Gross Margin to cover overhead and, therefore, serve the owner's dream lifestyle.

2. Product B appears to be the clear winner in the profitability category. It contributes a total Gross Profit of $120,000, and it has the highest Gross Margin (at 50%). So while its total sales are less than Product C, Product B actually produces more Gross Profit (in fact, it produces almost twice as much Gross Profit). But Product B's relatively low selling price of $8 means that the business must sell 30,000 of them to create that revenue.

   That volume may or may not be a problem. If a large amount of effort is required to create each sale and deal with the customers afterward, that will require a lot of time and resources from the business and its team (perhaps too much). However, if Product B is the type of product that is added to an existing sale (i.e., the extended warranties offered whenever you buy an electronic item these days), it's a great little product to promote.

3. Now let's take a look at Product A. It has a Gross Margin of 27%, and generated Gross Profit of $48,600 during the year. That would lead many business owners to think that this product is less desirable to sell. They would not view this product as the key to increasing the profit and cash flow they get from their business.

While sales of Product A clearly generated a smaller Gross Profit than Product C, the business only needed to sell 12,000 units of Product A, compared to 16,684 of Product C, and 30,000 of Product B.

Big deal?

Maybe. This analysis shows that Product A requires less "activity" (defined as product sales volume). And that usually means less effort and less overhead is required to create those sales (we will talk more about the impact of activities on Gross Profit later in this book).

So, putting all these issues together, which product is the best one for the business to focus on selling? Exhibit 7.6 shows a quick summary of our analysis to consider before we make any decision.

Item	Sales Price ($)	Cost ($)	Gross Margin (%)	Units Sold
A	15	11	$4 (27%)	12,000
B	8	4	$4 (50%)	30,000
C	19	15	$4 (21%)	16,684

Exhibit 7.6 Summary of Gross Margin for each product.

Again, I ask you: Which product should the business focus on selling?

That's actually a trick question. The answer is that we really don't know and can't effectively answer that question right now.

Why?

Remember, to actually make money, your business must do three things simultaneously. Remember what those three things are? Just to refresh your memory, they are:

1. Generate a positive net profit

2. Generate an adequate Return on Investment

3. Generate positive cash flow

For a product or service to make money for your business, it must do all three of these things too (it must have its own Triple Overlap). So far, our Gross Margin Analysis has only looked at the first criteria, profitability. If that's all we focus on, we could be setting ourselves up for a total disaster.

So, next we need to consider . . .

Gross Margin ROI

To understand how much money each product will create for your business, you must also consider the ROI of each product and service. To do that, you need to look at how much profit each product contributes relative to the investment in assets it requires. So, now that we've looked at the profitability of each product in the example, let's look at the ROI for each product.

Looking back at Exhibit 7.5 again, you can see that Product A has an inventory turnover of 73 days. This means that it takes about two and a half months to sell all its inventory one time, which causes the business to have roughly $26,250 of cash tied up in inventory of Product A at any one time.

This product also has an accounts receivable turnover (how quickly amounts owed to it by customers are paid) of 37 days. As a result, the business has roughly $18,000 in accounts receivable related to Product A at any one time.

To determine the total average investment in assets required by Product A, combine both those amounts (average inventory of $26,250 and average accounts receivable of $18,000). The total investment required by Product A, therefore, is $44,250.

When the total Gross Profit for Product A ($48,600) is compared to the total investment required ($44,250), the ROI for Product A is calculated. It is 110%.

Doing the same ROI calculations for all three products gives us the following results:

$$\text{Product A ROI} = \$48,600/(\$26,250 + \$18,000)$$

$$= 110\%$$

$$\text{Product B ROI} = \$120,000/(\$113,000 + \$85,000)$$

$$= 61\%$$

$$\text{Product C ROI} = \$66,570/(\$30,000 + \$100,000)$$

$$= 51\%$$

These values describe the relationship between the Gross Margin of each product and the investment in inventory and accounts receivable required to support it. For example, Product B's ROI of 61% tells us that for every $0.61 in Gross Margin, the business will require $1.00 in accounts receivable and inventory (assets that consume cash) to support it.

By dividing the percentages above into 1.00, the relationship becomes even clearer. When we do that, we get what I call the Gross Margin Support (GMS). The GMS tells you how much money must be invested in assets to support $1 in Gross Margin for any particular product or service. The GMSs for these three products are as follows:

$$\text{Product A GMS} = \$48,600/(\$26,250 + \$18,000)$$

$$= 110\%$$

$$= 1.0/110\%$$

$$= \$0.91$$

$$\text{Product B GMS} = \$120,000/(\$113,000 + \$85,000)$$

$$= 61\%$$

$$= 1.0/61\%$$

$$= \$1.65$$

$$\text{Product C GMS} = \$66,570/(\$30,000 + \$100,000)$$

$$= 51\%$$

$$= 1.0/51\%$$

$$= \$1.95$$

Product B, we see, has a GMS of $1.65. That means that for every $1.00 in Gross Profit produced from this product, the business will need to have $1.65 invested in inventory and accounts receivable.

Do you see anything wrong with that?

If all else remains the same and the business does not improve its ROI for Product B, it has a problem. If sales of Product B are increased, gross profit will increase. But the business will be starved for cash. Given the current situation in the business, Product B will suck up more cash (investment in inventory and accounts receivable) than is created by the additional gross profit.

That's not too much of a problem if the situation is temporary, the business owner sees what is going to happen, and has planned to secure cash from some other source (personal funds, bank loan, etc.). But it's going to be deadly if the owner doesn't see what is about to happen and continues to happily market away, trying to drive up sales of Product B because it creates a high Gross Profit. The owner is going to be absolutely blindsided by the cash shortage. And in the midst of the crisis and chaos that will result, the owner will look around and wonder what on Earth the problem is.

Found Money Rule of Product ROI and Gross Margin Support

Any product or service that has a Gross Margin Support of greater than 1.00 will produce negative cash flow EVERY time it is sold.

The corollary of that rule is that any product or service that has a Gross Margin Support greater than 1.00 needs triage. Action should be taken quickly to fix the situation, either by increasing Gross Margin (discussed later) or by reducing the investment in inventory and accounts receivable required.

Gross Margin Cash Flow

The final element in the Triple Overlap is positive cash flow.

Cash flow is fairly easy to calculate and track at an overall business level (though, surprisingly, it is often not done by business owners). Tracking cash flow at the overall business level basically consists of measuring historical cash flows. It's just a measurement of past history.

At the individual product or service level, however, it can be much more difficult to get a handle on cash flow. But one incredibly powerful tool can be used to measure and predict cash flow, as well as measure the Triple Overlap consequences in your business. It's a proxy for cash flow and can be calculated (okay, *must* be calculated) at the product level. This tool is actually something that can predict cash impacts of individual products and services.

What is this mystical beast? Its name is Working Capital Margin (WCM).

Working Capital Margin

The WCM for a product or service works similarly to the Gross Margin ROI, which we covered in the previous section. The difference is that WCM compares the total investment in assets required by a particular product or service to the total sales volume for the product or service. Gross Margin ROI, on the other hand, compared gross profit for a particular product to the total investment required by that product or service.

Once this number has been calculated, we'll do something very special with it, which you will see shortly.

The formula for WCM is:

$$\textbf{WCM} = \frac{(\textbf{Average Accounts Receivable} + \textbf{Average Inventory})}{\textbf{Sales}}$$

Using this formula, the WCMs for Products A, B, and C, which we've been beating to death (but only for a little longer, I promise) are calculated as follows:

Product A WCM = ($26,250 + $18,000)/$180,000

= 25%

$$\text{Product B WCM} = (\$113,000 + \$85,000)/\$240,000$$

$$= 83\%$$

$$\text{Product C WCM} = (\$30,000 + \$100,000)/\$317,000$$

$$= 41\%$$

What Does It Mean?

By itself, WCM doesn't really provide an awful lot of information for better decision making. But as soon as it is compared to Gross Margin Percentage (Gross Margin as a percentage of sales), it becomes dynamite.

Let's continue with our example and see just what's so wonderful about WCM, and what kind of tricks it can do for you. When we do a quick comparison of the Gross Margin and Working Capital Margin for each product, it looks like the results in Exhibit 7.7.

Product	Gross Margin (%)	Working Capital (%)
A	27%	25%
B	50%	83%
C	21%	41%

Exhibit 7.7 Gross Margin and Working Capital Margin comparison.

What does this really tell us?

Glad you asked.

Gross Margin (%), which we've already talked about in depth, indicates how much of every dollar in sales of a product or service will be left over to cover overhead, expand your business, and serve your dream lifestyle.

Working Capital Margin (%) indicates how much of every dollar in sales must be invested in accounts receivable and inventory.

Read the two previous paragraphs again and see if you pick up on their *huge* significance.

> ### Found Money Rule of Product Cash Flow and Working Capital Margin
>
> A rule to consider when thinking about your marketing efforts, and how to increase your business.
>
> Any product or service that has a Working Capital Margin (%) that is higher than its Gross Margin (%) will produce negative cash flow *every* time it is sold.

Please read that again. It's an absolute jaw-dropper when it clicks.

In other words, going back to our three different products, any efforts to sell more Product B and Product C will create a situation that requires additional cash to fund the increased sales. *Only* Product A can be sold without requiring additional cash.

The truly frightening thing is that almost every single business owner I have met, talked to, or worked with over the years would have missed the impact of the Triple Overlap analysis done in this chapter. They simply wouldn't have seen the disaster they were creating from their own efforts. Based on the Gross Margin of the three products and a failure to understand the Triple Overlap at the product level, these owners would have picked Product B (most of them), or maybe Product C. And then the owners who made those choices would have promoted, marketed, and sold that product with all their might in an attempt to make more money in the business.

But that very action would have *always* left the business short on cash and needing another cash injection. The owner would have struggled to get any money out of the business for their efforts (and forget about trying to live that dream lifestyle!). The final tragedy is that the owner would never realize the cause of the disaster he or she created through a lack of understanding of the Triple Overlap. The owner would have thrown their hands in the air and blamed the economy or heavy competition for the failure. Sadly, it would have been the owner's own blindness to the Triple Overlap that would be the source of the misery.

It's a tragedy that most business owners don't realize the importance of the Triple Overlap at the product level and know how to use it. Because not knowing can be fatal to their business, their dream lifestyle, and their financial and emotional health.

PUTTING THE TRIPLE OVERLAP TOGETHER

Whoooo-eeee!

We've covered a ton of stuff in this chapter so far. But be strong. It's almost over. Let's compare all three products we've been talking about, using all three elements of the Triple Overlap. Exhibit 7.8 gives a summary of what we now know.

	Product A	Product B	Product C
Gross Profit	$48,600	$120,000	$66,570
Gross Margin (%)	27%	50%	21%
ROI (%)	110%	61%	51%
WCM (%)	25%	83%	41%

Exhibit 7.8 Summary of product Triple Overlap.

When you look at all three products using the Triple Overlap, Product A is the clear winner even though it does not have the best gross profit or gross margin (%). But when it is analyzed (and compared to the other two products) using ROI and WCM (%) in addition to Gross Margin—in other words, using the Triple Overlap—it shines. It produces more gross profit for the money invested in inventory and accounts receivable. It is also the only one of the three products that can produce an increase in volume (gross profit) without demanding an additional cash investment to fund the increase. In fact, given the current situation of the business, it is the *only* product that can create any additional cash for the owners.

So the Triple Overlap tells you that to truly make money, your business must focus on selling Product A. That's not what most business owners would choose to do. They would most likely rely on Gross Margin and Gross Profit alone, and be mislead into choosing Product B or Product C. And then they would market hard, create more customers and sales of Products B and C, and be even shorter on cash than before their vigorous marketing efforts. They would be forced to work harder to keep up with the increased activity they created. And they would have even less money in their bank account (or a bigger loan) than before.

Sound familiar?

Now you know how to apply the Triple Overlap to analyze your products and services. And from now on, you're only going to focus on selling products and services that will make money (from a Triple Overlap viewpoint) for your business. And hopefully, you will also focus on taking action to remix and rebalance your sales mix to maximize profit and cash flow.

In Chapter 8, you are going to make sure you understand the mechanics of Gross Margin. It's a short chapter, but an important one . . .

CHAPTER

8

GROSS MARGIN MATH

You have worked incredibly hard through the last several chapters. They were pretty intense, I'll admit. But they had some powerful things in them. Things that should change the way you look at your business and its products and services forever.

This chapter, by contrast, is really short. It's just a quick discussion of a common problem I've seen over the years when working with business owners and talking about Gross Margin. Since Gross Margin is so important to maximizing your profit and cash flow, I want to make sure you don't suffer from this common mistake.

CALCULATING GROSS MARGIN

You've learned about Gross Margin and how important it is and why it holds the key to maximizing the profit and cash flow from your business. Because it's so important, you must be absolutely clear about how to calculate Gross Margin.

I'm making a big deal out of this because I have often seen business owners get confused between two related but different things. They often confuse Gross Margin and Markup. Mixing up these two concepts will spell disaster for your efforts to create a business that will serve your dream lifestyle.

Gross Margin is the difference between the amount at which you sell your products and services and the direct costs of those products and services. You just learned about Gross Margin in Chapter 7, so it's probably (hopefully) still fresh in your mind.

Markup is the amount you need to increase the direct costs of a product or service to achieve a certain Gross Margin.

To drive home the difference, here's a little quiz for you. Get out a calculator, and answer each of the three questions below:

1. You buy something for $150, and want a target Gross Margin of 53%. What is the price at which you should sell it to hit your target Gross Margin?
   a. $229.50
   b. $250.00
   c. $319.00
   d. $517.00

2. You have a target Gross Margin of 42%, and you incur direct costs of $2,500 (wage costs for a professional service you deliver). What price should you charge your customer?
   a. $5,000.00
   b. $4,310.00
   c. $3,550.00
   d. $3,560.00

(Continued)

3. You are going to mark up your product by 65%. If it costs you $100, what is the Gross Margin you will make on the sale?

    a. 65.0%

    b. 42.7%

    c. 39.4%

    d. 100.0%

The answers to these questions are below. But before you look at them, please take the time to actually answer these questions.

Did you find it easy or tough?

Want to know the answers? They are:

Question 1: c. $319.00

Question 2: b. $4,310.00

Question 3: c. 39.4%

Is that what you answered?

Don't worry if you got any (or all of them) wrong.

I have found that the answers business owners *usually* give (although they're wrong) are:

Question 1: a. $229.50 (but this would only provide a Gross Margin of 35% instead of the target of 53% Gross Margin)

Question 2: c. $3,550.00 (but this would only provide a Gross Margin of 30%, instead of the targeted 42% Gross Margin)

Question 3: a. 65.0%

Now you see how easy, and how common, it is to make the dangerous mistake between Markup and Gross Margin.

To make sure you never make this mistake, here's the formula for calculating the correct amount to mark something up, given a target Gross Margin:

$$\textbf{Markup Required} = \frac{\textbf{Cost of Goods Sold}}{\textbf{(1 − Target Gross Margin Percent)}}$$

Don't get caught *ever* making that mistake. It can be disastrous to your business and your dream lifestyle.

CHAPTER

9

WHICH CUSTOMERS MAKE YOU MONEY?
(And Which Ones Don't?)

You now understand that the Triple Overlap is the key to creating a business that makes you money. And you understand that the Triple Overlap must also be applied to each product and service your business sells if it is to create the profit, fun, and free time required for your dream lifestyle.

But guess what?

You now must turn your attention to applying the Triple Overlap to your *customers*, as well.

To effectively analyze which of your customers (or which major type of customer) make money for your business, you will turn once again to that "old friend" Gross Margin (I told you Gross Margin would form a foundation for the rest of the Found Money system, didn't I?). But in this chapter, those concepts are applied to your customers, rather than to your products and services.

MONEYMAKING CUSTOMERS

To know which of your customers actually make money for you, and which actually cost you money, you will first need to gather certain data. For each customer (or major category of customer if you've simply got too many) you need some key information. You need to know how much of each product or service they purchased from you, how much they paid for each of those products or services, the cost of sales (direct costs) for those products and services, and how much money they owed your business at any given time.

Let's start with a simple example to demonstrate how the Triple Overlap is applied to customers. Assume your business has the data shown in Exhibit 9.1 for your customers.

	Customer A	Customer B	Customer C
Units of Product A	25	10	0
Revenue from Product A	$375	$150	$0
Gross Margin Product A	33%	33%	33%
Gross Profit Product A	$125	$50	$0
Units of Product B	0	15	30
Revenue from Product B	$0	$120	$240
Gross Margin Product B	50%	50%	50%
Gross Profit Product B	$0	$60	$120
Units of Product C	5	35	65
Revenue from Product C	$95	$665	$1,235
Gross Margin Product C	21%	21%	21%
Gross Profit Product C	$20	$140	$261
Total Gross Profit	$145	$250	$381
Gross Profit Percentage	31%	27%	26%
Avg. Accounts Receivable	$55	$75	$250

Exhibit 9.1 Data for customer Triple Overlap.

This is a simple example, because it assumes only three customers. Don't let the simplicity fool you into glossing over this part. The lessons you are about to learn can be applied, with tremendous success, to any business with any number of customers.

So, based on this simple example, which customer is the most profitable for your business? Can you tell?

I'll give you a hint: The answer is "no." There's simply no way to know at this point. We have to do some analysis before we can correctly answer that question. Following the thinking behind the Triple Overlap, you want to examine your customers for their profitability to your business, as well as some measure of their "ROI" and "cash flow."

That's what we will be exploring in this chapter. Let's start by looking at customer profitability.

CUSTOMER GROSS PROFIT

Let's start our analysis by looking at Gross Profit for each customer. Customer C is the clear winner in this category. This customer generated a total Gross Profit of $381 for our business. The Gross Profit percentage they produced was 26%.

Customer A, on the other hand, only generated a Gross Profit of $145. The Gross Profit percentage for Customer A is 31%, compared to the 26% for Customer C.

Customer B fell between the other two, with a Gross Profit of $250 on sales revenue of $935, for a 27% Gross Profit percentage.

A False Conclusion

Remember the three things your business needs to do to make you money? Please tell me you remember. It must make an adequate net profit, have an adequate ROI, and provide positive cash flow, right?

The same thing applies for your customers. The terms are slightly different, but the same three concepts (the Triple Overlap) still apply. So that means the customer Gross Profit is only one element of a moneymaking customer.

Failing to look at customers using all three elements of the Triple Overlap usually leads to false, dangerous, and sometimes fatal decisions. This is a clear area where a little knowledge really *is* a dangerous thing.

For example, relying only on the analysis of customer profitability done so far would lead many business owners to the conclusion that Customer C is the most profitable. Because of that, they would focus most of their efforts on dealing with, and trying to get more, C-type customers.

That conclusion is correct, as far as Gross Profit goes. After all, Customer C did earn the business the most gross profit, at $381. That amount is more than 50% higher than the next highest customer (Customer B). But that's definitely not the entire story.

CUSTOMER ROI

Next we will consider the second element of making money (an adequate Return on Investment). We're going to follow the same concepts as when we looked at ROI for a business as a whole, and for individual products and services. There are some minor differences when we apply those concepts to customers, but the concept remains steadfast.

For customer ROI, we need to compare the Gross Profit generated by a customer to the investment in assets demanded by that customer. Since it is almost impossible to get an accurate measure of how much inventory is associated with a particular customer, it is usually practical to simplify the measurement of customer ROI by looking at the level of accounts receivable (A/R) demanded by different customers.

In our example, the average accounts receivable for Customer C was the highest by far ($250, compared to $55 for Customer A and $75 for Customer B) Even though Customer C was making the business a nice Gross Profit, he or she was also tying up a lot more of the business's money. In fact, Customer C required an investment in accounts receivable that was slightly higher than 4.5 times the amount needed by Customer A and slightly higher than 3.3 times the amount required for Customer B.

When we calculate the Customer ROI (using the formula Gross Profit/Accounts Receivable), we get the results shown in Exhibit 9.2.

	Customer A	Customer B	Customer C
Gross Profit	$145	$250	$381
Accounts Receivable	$55	$75	$250
ROI (%)	263%	334%	152%

Exhibit 9.2 Customer ROI comparison.

Customer ROI for Fun and Profit

What does this mean from a practical point of view?

Let's look at a little scenario.

Suppose your current marketing efforts were directed at attracting more customers just like Customer C. After all, you reasoned, Customer C creates the largest gross profit for your business.

Operating under that assumption, you create a marketing strategy that brings in four more customers just like Customer C. That means your business would generate additional gross profit of $1,524 from the marketing effort ($381 gross profit multiplied by 4 new C-type customers).

But getting those four new customers would require you to invest an additional $1,000, because of the average $250 A/R balance these customers carry. Let's assume that you have had the foresight to anticipate this increase in accounts receivable, and you have the cash flow in place (although you'd be amazed at how many business owners attack their marketing without any consideration of the demand that may be placed on cash flow; that's because they don't understand the Triple Overlap. But, you're oh, so different, right?).

The real question to ask to find all the hidden profit and cash flow is whether the business could have done better with the same investment of effort in marketing and the same $1,000 in cash.

Maybe. Let's look at what else you could do with that $1,000.

Based on the information presented, that same $1,000 could support the addition of 18 more A-type customers (compared to only four more C-type customers). This is because each "Customer A" only requires an investment in A/R of $55.

That means even though each A-type customer only generates total gross profit of $145, if you attracted 18 of them (which is how many your business could support using the same $1,000 investment), your marketing efforts would create an additional total gross profit of $2,610 (18 × $145).

That's an overall improvement of $1,086, compared to the option of attracting four C-type customer. And that additional $1,086 is realized on the investment of $1,000 to support those customers. That's more than a 100% additional return on that $1,000 cash investment!

The same analysis can (and should) be done for Customer B. Each Customer B requires the business to invest $75 in A/R. That means the same $1,000 could support 13 more B-type customers.

Using the average gross profit of $250 for Customer B, adding 13 more of these customers would generate an additional $3,250 in gross profit. That's $1,726 more than the additional gross profit that four new C-type customers would offer.

Exhibit 9.3 is a table that summarizes what we've just talked about.

	Customer A	Customer B	Customer C
Additional Accounts Receivable	$1,000	$1,000	$1,000
Number of New Customers	18	13	4
Gross Profit / Customer	$145	$250	$381
Total Increased Gross Profit	$2,610	$3,250	$1,524

Exhibit 9.3 Potential increased Gross Profit comparison.

You will notice that Customer B has the highest potential Gross Profit increase, given a fixed additional investment in accounts receivable. And Customer B also has the highest ROI. Compared to simply looking at the Gross Profit of each customer, a very different picture is emerging. Maybe Customer C isn't your best marketing target.

Before you decide where to aim your efforts at maximizing profit and cash flow, however, you need to complete the picture by analyzing customers using the third element of the Triple Overlap.

CUSTOMER CASH FLOW

In Chapter 7, on analyzing which products made the most money for your business, you were introduced to the concept of Working Capital Margin (WCM). Now you're going to apply the same thinking and strategy to what I call the Customer Capital Margin (CCM).

This is a unique measurement designed to approximate the amount of cash flow associated with a specific customer. Since true cash flow occurs at the business level, it is impossible to easily and elegantly measure the true cash flow for any one customer. So the CCM measure is used to provide a simple, yet effective, estimate.

CCM compares the investment required for each customer (their demand on cash flow) to the revenue generated by that customer.

The formula for CCM is shown in Exhibit 9.4.

$$CCM = \frac{\text{Accounts Receivable} + \text{Inventory}}{\text{Sales}}$$

Exhibit 9.4 Customer Capital Margin formula.

If you're really on the ball, you feel like you've seen that formula somewhere before. It's exactly the same as the formula for WCM, except it's done at the individual customer level, rather than at the product level. As a practical matter, the investment in inventory isn't used, because it is usually far too difficult to reasonably determine how much inventory is required to service a particular customer.

Now let's jump in and see how the three customers look using this measure, as shown in Exhibit 9.5.

	Customer A	Customer B	Customer C
Average Accounts Receivable	$55	$75	$250
Sales	$470	$935	$1,475
CCM	12%	8%	17%

Exhibit 9.5 Customer Capital Margin comparison.

CCM by itself isn't that useful. Like the WCM, its real power is revealed when it is compared to the Gross Profit (%) for a particular customer. In Exhibit 9.6, you will see the same table you just looked at, with the addition of the Gross Profit information.

	Customer A	Customer B	Customer C
Average Accounts Receivable	$55	$75	$250
Sales	$470	$935	$1,475
CCM	12%	8%	17%
Gross Profit (%)	31%	27%	26%

Exhibit 9.6 Customer Capital Margin and Gross Profit comparison.

Just as with the WCM analysis in Chapter 7, as long as the CCM (%) is not higher than the Gross Profit (%), cash flow should be positive. And it stands to reason that the lower the CCM is for a particular customer, the better the cash flow that particular customer will generate.

CCM'S COOL, BUT CAN IT MAKE YOU MONEY?

How can you use CCM, from a practical standpoint, to make better business decisions? To answer that question, we will take another look at the customer data in our simple table above.

To conduct our demonstration, assume that you are currently targeting your marketing efforts to attract more C-type customers. After all, you reason, these are the customers who create the largest gross profit for your business.

Operating under that assumption, you create a marketing strategy that brings in 10 more C-type customers. Your total sales revenue would increase by $14,750 (revenue of $1,475 per Customer C × 10 new C-type customers).

Most business owners would think that was wonderful. And it might be. But to really know if that result is a good one, you need to do a little bit of analysis, using the CCM. If you don't, you can't really draw an accurate conclusion.

Referring to the table in Exhibit 9.6, you can see that the CCM for a Customer C is 17%. That means for every $100 of revenue earned from such a customer, your business must invest $17 in A/R to support that revenue. So in our example, the additional $14,750 of revenue would require about $2,500 of additional investment in A/R.

We also know from the data provided that a single Customer C gives the business a gross profit of $381. That means 10 new C-type customers would give a total additional gross profit of $3,810. Not a bad return on the incremental investment of $2,500.

But as good as that may seem, the real issue is whether the business could have done any better by understanding and applying CCM. To do that, you need to consider whether the business could have done better, using the same investment in marketing and the same $2,500 investment required for the 10 new C-type customers.

Based on the data for this business, the $2,500 investment in A/R for C-type customers could support additional sales of $20,833 to A-type customers. This number is arrived at by dividing the $2,500 by the CCM (12% for Customer A). When the total additional Customer A revenue that $2,500 could support is compared to the average sale for this customer, we calculate that the $2,500 investment could support 44 new A-type customers (divide the additional revenue of $20,833 by the average sale of $470).

Following our chain of logic a little bit further (don't leave me, damn it!), the $145 gross profit produced by a single Customer A would create a new total gross profit of $6,380 (44 new customers × $145).

The same analysis done for Customer B would look like this:

Customer B Revenue supported = $2,500/8%
= $31,250
Number of B-type customers = $31,250/$935
= 33 Customer B's B-type customers
Total Gross Profit from new Bs = 33 × $250
= $8,250

Exhibit 9.7 gives a summary of this CCM analysis.

	Customer A	Customer B	Customer C
Additional Accounts Receivable	$2,500	$2,500	$2,500
Number of New Customers	44	33	10
Gross Profit per Customer	$145	$250	$381
Total Increased Gross Profit	$6,380	$8,250	$3,810

Exhibit 9.7 Customer Capital Margin analysis.

This type of analysis often surprises business owners the first time I go through it with them. In fact, I've even had some pretty intense arguments over it. Compared to simply looking at customer profitability, this analysis provides a shockingly different picture. Customer C, which provides the largest gross profit per customer, isn't the best target once CCM is factored into the equation.

Relying purely on the Gross Profit of each customer (remember the Danger Zone discussion early in the book?) rather than applying the Triple Overlap methodology would set the business owner up for a wreck. Looking at Gross Profit alone would lead the owner to market to C-type customers in the hope of attracting as many of them as possible. That goal would be based on the seductive, but entirely false and dangerous, assumption that the large gross profit from more C-type customers would lead to more money for the owner.

The tragedy is that the very belief that is most seductive would actually reduce the money (cash flow) created for the owners. They would find themselves working harder and actually making less money because the business would be demanding more cash than before. They would end up hurt, emotionally drained, physically tired, and financially damaged, despite their best intentions and misplaced analysis. And they would blame the economy, their competitors, and anything else they could think of, because they really had no idea how it really happened. Sadly, such a dismal situation could have easily been avoided by knowing and using the Triple Overlap and the Found Money system and tools.

10

YOUR CUSTOMER PROFITABILITY MAP

I like to think of each business as being a lot like a castle, like the ones you see in old movies. In those movies, the castle was created by the king (actually, he envisioned it, and then used skilled people to actually do the heavy work, but no matter), and it was the king who decided who would be allowed to come inside the castle walls.

At the same time, there were always hostile forces who wanted to get inside the castle, take it over, and change the peaceful existence maintained by the ruler.

To defend against unwanted people coming in (either hostile or simply undesirable), the castles had walls to keep people out, and a drawbridge to strictly control who could get inside. The only ones who gained access were people the ruler liked and wanted to have inside with him.

The drawbridge was the access point that was used to control who was allowed inside and who was prevented from entering.

YOUR VERY OWN DRAWBRIDGE

In your business, you also have a drawbridge that can be used to determine who gets inside. You can control who gets the privilege of working with you and your team, if you have the courage to exercise that control.

And if you have any hopes of building a business that maximizes your profit, fun, and free time and serves your dream lifestyle, you simply *must* exercise that control. Get used to it, because your ultimate success, happiness, and lifestyle depend upon it.

For example, a recent article in *Condé Nast Portfolio* magazine told a story about the restaurant chain Carl's Jr. In a time when emphasis on healthy alternatives has increased at most fast food chains, Carl's Jr. has done just the opposite. As the article points out:

> In an age when other chains have been forced to at least pretend that they care about the health of their customers ... Hardee's and Carl's Jr. are purposely running in the opposite direction, unapologetically creating an arsenal of higher-priced, high-fat, high-calorie monstrosities—pioneering avant-garde concepts such as "meat as condiment" and "fast-food porn"—and putting the message out to increasingly receptive consumers with ads that are often as controversial as the burgers themselves."[1]

Carl's Jr. has focused its marketing and business efforts to attract and retain a very specific type of customer—a customer who wants a totally decadent, delicious, over-the-top, "damn the health police" fast food experience.

Everything Carl's Jr. does is designed to get those specific customers through their doors and to keep the "healthy fast food" customers out. They simply aren't desirable to Carl's Jr's business model, and the company has the courage to unapologetically admit it.

---

[1] *Condé Nast Portfolio*; February, 2008; "Fat Profits" by Joe Kahane.

YOUR CUSTOMER PROFITABILITY MAP

How do you decide who *you* should let into *your* business? After all, like the old castles, there are many different people trying to get inside. And if you don't consciously decide who has access, you're going to find your business overrun with barbarians (okay, maybe not quite that bad, but you certainly won't have control over your business and its destiny).

To help decide who you should let inside your business and who should be kept out, I have developed a useful and valuable tool. It should be used as a fundamental step before you undertake any major marketing or business-building effort. I've named this tool . . . (drumroll, please) . . . the Customer Profitability Map.

The Customer Profitability Map (CPM) is a way of sorting and ranking the customers for any business. The CPM Analysis allows any business owner and their team to quickly uncover vital information that will help drive the business toward becoming one that serves their dream lifestyle.

The ranking is done using two criteria. The first one is the profitability of each customer. This is a numeric fact that you obtain from your business records. The second criterion is a subjective one that I've called the Resonance Score.

We will discuss these two criteria in more detail soon, but first let me give you a big-picture example to convince you to pay attention to this stuff.

An Example of the Customer Profitability Map

Assume that you own a company, and you have hired me to help you understand where the business should focus its efforts to maximize profit, cash flow, fun, and free time. As part of the process I have asked you to rank all your customers according to their profitability and their Resonance Score (you are going to find out a lot more about Resonance Scores, what they are, and how to do them very shortly, so don't worry about the new term at this moment).

Exhibit 10.1 shows what your customer base looks like when it's plotted using those two criteria.

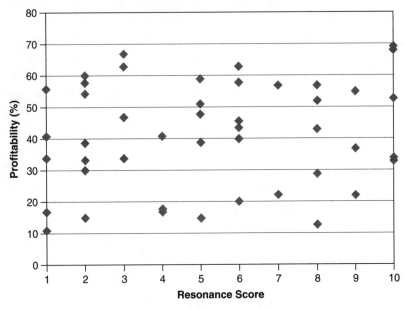

Exhibit 10.1 Customer Profitability plot.

So what? What's so special about that? It's just an ugly plot of a bunch of dots, right?

Absolutely correct. It's useless!

But the good news is that this isn't the Customer Profitability Map (CPM); it's only the *first step* in creating the CPM.

If we go on to assign some categories to this chart, and give it some meaning, we will quickly convert this data set into an incredibly revealing CPM.

Before we do that, let's stop and consider what the data that has been plotted is actually saying.

The scale on the left shows the profitability of each customer. The closer to the top of the chart a customer is, the more profitable that customer is to the business.

For example, a customer with a profitability score of 70% would create $700 of profit for the business for every $1,000 they purchased.

Likewise, a customer with a profitability of 20% would only result in a profit of $200 for the business for the same $1,000 sale.

The scale across the bottom of the chart shows each customer's Resonance Score. This is a score of between 1 and 10 that you give each of your customers, capturing how well they fit in with your business, your team, and your approach to business. It attempts to rank how pleasant it is to work with that customer.

RESONANCE SCORE

The Resonance Score is such a fundamental element of the CPM that it deserves extra attention to make sure you fully understand both the score and how to determine it.

The Resonance Score is a subjective number between 1 and 10 that you give each customer, based on things such as:

- How pleasant they are to deal with

- How much they respect you and your team

- How respectful of your time (and that of your team) they are

- Whether their expectations and demands of your business are reasonable

- Whether they are "fun" to deal with

- Whether they allow you, your team, and your business to use your full talents

- Whether they treat you as equals or as servants

The Resonance Score is a subjective measure of the "gut feeling" you and your team have about how well a particular customer clicks with your business.

Customers who achieve a higher score are the ones with whom you find business much more pleasant. These customers value you, your team, and what your business does for them.

BACK TO THE CUSTOMER PROFITABILITY PLOT

So let's return to the plot of the customer data we looked at previously. If we take this data and break it into four distinct quadrants, we will get the chart that follows in Exhibit 10.2.

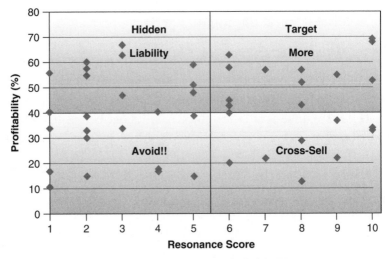

Exhibit 10.2 Customer Profitability Map.

This is the Customer Profitability Map (CPM)! I've named each quadrant—Hidden Liability, Avoid!, Cross-Sell, and Target More—to help describe the impact customers in that part of the map have on your business and their relevance to creating your dream lifestyle. Each name is designed both to describe the customers who fall into each quadrant and to serve as a reminder for you whenever you think about your business and your customers.

Now let's put the customers that fall into each quadrant into perspective.

Hidden Liability

These customers are quite profitable for your business. However, they have low Resonance Scores.

In other words, while they do generate a good profit for the business, that profit comes at a fairly high price. And that price is reflected in their low Resonance Scores.

Perhaps these customers are too demanding, put unrealistic and unfair demands on you and your team, or are chronically grumbling about prices, service, your team, and whatever else they can. No matter the reason, the fact that these customers have a low Resonance Score suggests they really don't "click" with you, your business, and your team.

These are the type of customers who "always feel like work." You know the feeling; it just always seems that they aren't truly valuing your business, its products, its services, or your team. And it always feels unnatural or unpleasant to deal with them. There's just no connection.

Their category is given the name *Hidden Liability* because they represent a hidden danger for your business. Due to their low Resonance Scores, it is likely that they will switch to another competitive business as soon as they see the opportunity, or find something that they perceive to be better. The fact that they will ultimately leave your business isn't a bad thing. Remember, their low Resonance Scores generally make them emotionally draining and difficult to serve.

But the fact that they are also highly profitable is what creates the *Hidden Liability*. Because when they do finally switch to a competitor, the business loses a significant amount of profit along with them. And that "profit hole" is what gives rise to the *Hidden Liability*.

They are a chunk of profit just waiting to evaporate from your business. And that's not a good thing, is it?

Avoid!

Customers in this quadrant are those who don't really have anything going for them. Okay, that's probably a bit harsh—but it's true, from the point of view of the Customer Profitability Map. After all, they are among the least profitable customers, *and* they have low Resonance Scores.

In other words, not only are they a pain to deal with (low Resonance Scores), they aren't even worth the effort! They aren't profitable for the business.

Customers (and prospects) who fall into this quadrant are absolute poison to your business.

They can bog your business down under a punishing load of low-profit work, strangling your business and your team to the point where you can't take care of the clients who really do make you money and have high Resonance Scores. These customers can hijack your business, holding your profit, fun, and free time hostage.

Your success, happiness, and dream lifestyle absolutely demand that you do everything in your power to make sure you *don't* deal with these people. Don't let them in your front door. Don't waste a minute of time or an ounce of effort trying to attract or even talk to these people.

And if you've got any of them as customers right now (every business, sadly, has many), *get rid of them*. These are the people who must never be allowed to get past your drawbridge. If you find any of these people inside your business, toss them out.

And toss them out immediately!

Cross-Sell

This quadrant represents a ton of potential for your business and your dream lifestyle.

Customers in this quadrant are a true delight. They have high Resonance Scores. And that means they enjoy your business, respect you and your team, and generally have a pleasant working relationship with your business.

They sound like a dream, and when it comes to clicking with you, your business, and your team, they really are. But they aren't perfect, by any stretch. At least for now.

The dirty little secret these customers hide (but not any longer, because you've found them out) is that they aren't very profitable.

But guess what?

They don't have to stay unprofitable.

The fact that these customers have a high Resonance Score means you have a real opportunity to convert them into much more profitable customers—and that's true for any business.

The established relationship and connection these customers have with the business is a good one (that's why they have high Resonance Scores). And that provides a huge opportunity to cross-sell them additional products and services that the business might be able to provide. In many cases, it quickly becomes apparent that these customers were completely unaware of all the additional products and services the business could offer.

Target More

These are the jewel-box clients for your business. These people have a great relationship with the business and its team members, and they value its products and services (i.e., they have a high Resonance Score). In addition to that, they generate a generous profit for the business.

Hmmmmm.

Let's see: fun to deal with *and* profitable.

We want more of these customers!

GUARD YOUR DRAWBRIDGE

Okay, now we've categorized the customers for this business and identified the characteristics that cause any particular customer to fall into a particular quadrant. Because of that, it's suddenly easy to effectively plan and execute various tactics to move the business toward becoming one that serves your dream lifestyle.

Because the characteristics of the customers in each category are different, the strategies and tactics used for each category should be (in fact *must* be) different. The goals for each category are different. And that means each of these customer categories requires different techniques and approaches.

Building your dream lifestyle and creating a business that maximizes your profit, fun, and free time depends on this.

Remember, not everyone deserves to get past your drawbridge. And not everyone who has managed to get in deserves to stay inside.

It's your business.

Act like it.

CUSTOMER PROFITABILITY MAP TACTICS AND ACTIONS

Now that you've put each of your customers into a context for evaluating them, you are in a great position to take specific actions for each different type of customer. Individual actions and tactics for each business will depend on the exact nature of the business, the owner's dream lifestyle goals, and the nature and distribution of the customers.

But there are some common actions, or themes for action, that can (and should) be taken for all businesses.

Following are some examples of the broad types of actions that are most relevant for customers in each of the four categories. With these broad actions as guidelines, use your ingenuity and creativity, along with that of your team members, to come up with specific actions, plans and timelines.

Hidden Liability

The theme for customers in this quadrant is *"Find out what's wrong."*

These customers are profitable for your business, and you really must try to find out why they aren't a good fit with your business. Many times, customers in this quadrant simply have different expectations for their interaction with a business than the owners and team have.

Amazingly, customers in this quadrant can often be "converted" or "rehabilitated" into the *Target More* quadrant simply by discussing their expectations and being open about yours.

A great tool for finding out what's wrong is to use inexpensive customer advisory sessions or, perhaps, one-on-one meetings. These are sessions that bring in a small group of customers who fall into this quadrant. You tell customers how valuable they are to your business (because they truly are), and then tell them that because of their value, the business, its owners, and, its team members dearly want to find out how the customers can be better served, or how their experience with the business can be improved.

This type of tactic is quite inexpensive. It usually results in a greatly improved relationship with the customer (a higher Resonance Score) and often reveals amazing new product and service opportunities that had not yet been even imagined.

The effort almost always provides a tremendous return on the time and money required.

The things your customers tell you they don't like, when you run these sessions, are like gold to you. In the majority of cases, these issues turn out to be tiny things that are easily and quickly fixed. But don't trivialize them.

Even though they may be tiny things to you, to your customer they are tremendously important. And if you take the time to get them to tell you what they don't like and then fail to fix it, it puts you into a worse position than before you knew what was bothering them. Because now your customer knows you know.

So *do not* trivialize anything that these customers tell you.

It's always amazing to me to see how just a few small, simple changes identified in these sessions can literally transform a low Resonance Score customer into one with a high Resonance Score, almost instantly.

Avoid!

Tactics for these customers are easy.

Send each of them a letter explaining that the business has recently done some restructuring and, due to resource constraints, can't service all customers any longer. Then, suggest a couple of competitors for them to start using instead of your business.

That's right.

Fire these customers!

They take up too much time and emotional energy and contribute little, if any, profit to the business. They are dead wood, and need to be removed as soon as possible.

And if you can gum up your competition with a sudden influx of these customers, *they* (your competitors) will quickly become bogged down. Their attention will be drawn to dealing with the new "problem" customers, leaving their valuable customers vulnerable to being wooed by cunning old you.

Do it.

You and your team will feel like the greatest weight imaginable has just been lifted off your shoulders. And a huge weight really will have been removed—the useless weight of a bunch of customers from your *Avoid!* quadrant.

Cross-Sell

Tactics for dealing with customers in this quadrant are also easy and quite inexpensive.

After all, you already know these customers and have a connection with them. You get along great with them, and they click with the style and approach of your business (after all, their high Resonance Score is what qualifies them to be in this quadrant, isn't it?).

Plan to spend some time meeting with these customers. You can do this individually (a great idea for really significant customers), in small groups, or even in large "sponsored" groups (such as at a seminar or presentation).

The goal of these meetings is to make these customers aware of the entire range of products and services the business can provide—ones that these customers may not be currently using.

Regular communications, such as newsletters, blogs, seminars, and so forth, can also be used to keep in contact with these customers and keep them aware of all that the business can do.

Pricing must also be considered for these customers. In many cases, these customers are paying a price that is too low to provide an adequate margin for the business. Paradoxically, this is often due to the fact that they have high Resonance Scores. Their high scores often create a friendly or "buddy" relationship.

While that is a great thing, it can sometimes make business owners feel guilty about charging a high enough price. I've never understood that, but it happens quite a lot.

So make sure that the products and services these customers are currently buying are priced fairly and properly to return an adequate margin to your business.

Target More

You definitely want more of these customers,

These people have a high Resonance Score (so they are a great fit with the business) and they generate a high profit.

Let's see . . . profitable *and* fun.

Yep. These are the kinds of people you should really dig.

And this is the *only* category of customers that you should be willing to pay to increase.

What does that mean?

It means that you must review every one of your ads and marketing tactics (after all, these things are simply a way of swapping money for customers). Track the results to make sure that the customers that are generated by those efforts fall into this quadrant.

After all, if you are going to pay money to acquire customers, be selective in which customers you attract. No sense throwing money at advertising that yields only low-quality customers (i.e., customers who aren't in your Target More quadrant).

So spend time reviewing how these customers became *your* customers. What are the sources of new customers that fit into this quadrant? Do they come from a particular type of ad or media? Do they come from a particular referral source? Do they come from a particular type of networking activity?

Take the extra time and spend the extra money where necessary to ensure your efforts are hitting the right prospects (customers who are going to fall into this quadrant). Not doing that is like throwing money at the lottery. Sure, you might end up with some good customers, but the odds of that happening are really, really, really small.

Putting It Together

Now that customers in all four quadrants have been identified, it's time to do some analyzing. You want to identify some patterns and common characteristics of customers in each quadrant.

The goal is to uncover patterns that will start to give you control over the number of customers your business gets in each quadrant. Doing that will allow you to focus your marketing and business management efforts like a laser.

You should approach and interact with customers and prospects in each quadrant in a different way. Tailor the actions of your business and your team in a way that makes sense, given the different characteristics and value of each quadrant.

For example, if you note that most (or even many) of your customers in the *Avoid!* quadrant came to your business through the Yellow Pages, that's golden information. It doesn't mean that the Yellow Pages are not effective (because they absolutely are!). But that information does mean your Yellow Page ad is somehow not resonating with the right people. Or maybe it isn't qualifying them well enough.

You might want to consider a smaller Yellow Pages ad. Or even better, you could change the way your ad looks and what it says to better qualify (prequalify) prospects before they call in, and to resonate with the right prospects.

This is exactly what happened to me when I was building my first business several years ago. I did this type of analysis, and discovered that a series of ads I was running were generating clients who fell into one of two categories: either they were "price-only" buyers, or they were looking for an accountant that would allow them to do some "shady" transactions.

The "price-only" clients always seemed to think that nothing was fast enough, good enough, or cheap enough. They were a complete chore, and they sucked the joy and fun out of being in business.

The "shady" clients wanted an accountant who would look the other way and let certain transactions slide.

Neither type of those clients was going to provide a strong foundation for my business.

Once I realized the trend that was being generated by that ad, I changed it so it did a better job of qualifying the prospects who responded. And as soon as I did that, a lot less "price-only" and "shady" prospects stopped responding to my ads.

CREATING YOUR OWN CUSTOMER PROFITABILITY MAP

Now it's time to roll up your sleeves. You're going to dig into the detail of how to do a Customer Profitability Analysis for your own business.

The first step is to print out a list of all the customers who have done business with you within the last year. If a one-year cycle doesn't make sense for your business, then use a more appropriate time period.

If you've got thousands of customers, you should try grouping them in an appropriate manner, and then do your analysis for each major grouping. Another alternative, if you have way too many clients to analyze individually, is to select a sample that is representative of your overall client base.

However, if possible, it's definitely best to do the analysis individually. It's more work, and much more tedious, no doubt. But the more specific your analysis is, the better and more accurate information your Customer Profitability Map will provide. And you will get a much better feel for your population of customers.

The second step is to go through your accounting and customer records. For each customer (or grouping, if you've opted for that route), record the total sales for the last year. Don't record each individual sale, just a total of all their purchases from your business.

At this point in your analysis, you don't need to worry about breaking down customer sales into each different product or service. If you have set up your accounting and data files to track and report that information, it's a great way to go. But if you haven't (and many businesses don't track at that level—until they've been exposed to Found Money), stick to total sales. That will give you enough data to begin your analysis and identify your different quadrants.

Next, you're going to have to come up with the Cost of Goods Sold (COGS) for the total sales made to each customer. This cost will be the actual cost of the goods you had to purchase to resell to each customer for parts and materials that went into what you sold each customer, and staff wages to create or provide the products and services.

If you have set up your bookkeeping system to track these costs in this way that's wonderful—you've just saved yourself some work. If not, you should do it manually by going through some vendor invoices and employee timesheets to get a good estimate of these costs.

You also should try to come up with an estimate of the amount of time each customer required from you and your team in the process of making those purchases from your business during the year. That is, make the estimate if you've got an easy way to determine it. If not, don't worry. Customers who chew up a lot of time and administrative effort will most likely show up through low Resonance Scores, so it's likely that they will still be properly categorized.

If you run a service business, you will need to calculate the cost of creating those sales by calculating how much time was invested in generating the services each customer purchased. To come up with this cost, use the actual average wage cost (including payroll burden such as payroll taxes and employee benefits) for the team members who provided the services (*not* the "charge-out" rates, which are based on multiples of actual wage costs, professional service firms are so often addicted to).

The next step is to determine the profitability of each customer. This amount is simply the difference between the total sales each customer had with your business and the total COGS for those sales divided by each customer's total sales. The result is a Profit Percentage for each customer.

$$\text{Customer Profit Percentage} = \frac{(\text{Sales} - \text{COGS})}{\text{Sales}}$$

Now that you've identified each customer's profitability, assign a Resonance Score to each customer to go along with the Customer Profit Percentage. When assigning Resonance Scores, don't allow yourself to be swayed by profitability. Be objective. It's tough, but ask yourself (and your team) to try to accurately rate how "difficult" the relationship is between your business and each customer. This measure should be independent of how profitable each customer is.

The goal is for you and each member of your team to assign a subjective evaluation (on a scale of 1–10, where 1 is the worst, and 10 is an absolute delight) to each customer. It is important to have each member of your team do this. Business owners are often surprised to discover that the customers they thought would have high Resonance Scores actually are given low scores by the team. That usually indicates a particular customer doesn't value or respect the team and the business. They only value the owner. And that's important information to have.

The final step is to chart these customers on your own Customer Profitability Map. You can download a copy of the worksheet and use the online calculator to do your own Map by visiting the Found Money section at www.stevewilkinghoff.com.

ANALYZING YOUR CUSTOMER PROFITABILITY MAP

Now that you've created your Customer Profitability Map, it's time to start using it. You will now be able to really dial in your business. You're going to dig deep to uncover some potential problems and some hidden opportunities. This analysis will form the roadmap for you to really move your business toward becoming one that serves your dream lifestyle.

In a short period of time, you're going to know the following things about your business:

- How many customers your business is at risk of losing to a competitor

- How much of your profits would be likely to evaporate if your business faced any new competitive pressures

- How much of your profits are at risk if one of your existing competitors makes a sudden move in your marketplace

- How much extra profit a potential marketing tactic might generate (or should generate)

- What kind of realistic and measurable results you should demand from your marketing tactics

- Which of your existing marketing tactics should be continued, and which should be immediately stopped

It might sound a little bit like science fiction, but a careful analysis of your Customer Profitability Map can tell you all those things and more. Of course, there is a caveat. You will need to have created an accurate Customer Profitability Map. If you "fluffed" a bunch of data and didn't take the time to truly drill down into your business to get solid data (and I know that's a chore in some cases), your Customer Profitability Map is not going to be anything more than a cute exercise.

So if you haven't really dug deep and done your own Customer Profitability Map (perhaps you felt it was too much effort), stop reading now and do it before proceeding further in this book.

You should do four main analyses with your Customer Profitability Map. They are listed below, and will be discussed more fully in a few moments. For the moment, we're just going to list these analyses and give you a quick description of each one and what it does.

1. *Total Quadrant Weighting*. This shows the percentage of customers your business has in each of the four quadrants. It

provides a powerful graphic look at the risks and opportunities that currently exist in your business. This analysis serves as a starting point to clearly find out where your business is right now.

2. *Profit At Risk*. This measure provides an estimate of the amount of profit your business could lose quickly if faced with competitive attacks in your market. It's a rough estimate, because it uses the quadrant average, and there is no way of knowing exactly how much such a loss would be until it occurs. But it's still tremendously useful to know the size of this at-risk profit amount.

3. *Cross-Sell Potential*. This measure shows how much "early yardage" your business has waiting to be tapped. It shows the kind of hidden profits on which you could capitalize, quickly and easily, to generate profit and cash flow to sustain the rest of your change efforts. This measure relies on the fact that it's practically a guarantee that many of your customers could, and would, buy more things from you, if you only offered those things to them.

4. *Profit replacement potential*. This measure tells you how much new profit your business could create quickly by getting rid of customers in the *Avoid!* quadrant.

Why does analyzing your Customer Profitability Map matter to you?

Because you are *never* going to be able to realize the full potential of your business (by maximizing the profit, cash flow, fun and free time you get) if you don't do the analysis. Unless you just get plain lucky (which is very unlikely), it's going to be difficult, if not impossible, to transform your business to serve your dream lifestyle if you don't understand and apply Customer Profitability Mapping.

You have limited resources—time, money, emotional energy, staff, and so forth—in your business. Every business is faced with these limits. Your CPM provides an effective way to ensure you don't waste *any* of these scarce resources, and that you get the maximum benefit from their use.

An Example of a Customer Profitability Map Analysis

Let's look at a data set for a sample business to demonstrate how the analysis of a Customer Profitability Map works. The owners of this business, along with their team, have done the legwork and identified the profitability and a consensus Resonance Score for each of their customers. The information is as shown in Exhibit 10.3.

Customer	Profitability	Resonance Score	Customer	Profitability	Resonance Score
Smith	17%	4	Miles	53%	10
Bachmeir	43%	8	Michelow	22%	9
Avery	33%	10	Pentoski	22%	7
Varry	41%	4	Punter	69%	10
Beach	45%	6	Pyllieko	56%	1
Bihg	13%	8	Power	39%	5
Burpen	29%	8	Reynolds	52%	8
Buble	58%	6	Reimer	57%	7
Clark	51%	5	Rayphon	34%	3
Dallo	60%	2	Schneider	40%	6
Cross	43%	6	Sinclair	37%	9
Gladious	63%	6	Stewart	18%	4
Gibson	47%	3	Stimmer	48%	5
Gill	59%	5	White	41%	1
George	34%	1	Weimer	15%	2
Jones	68%	10	Young	11%	1
Kunder	17%	1	Zetmeyer	55%	9
Kraus	39%	2	Carlson	34%	10
Latintomak	20%	6	Howe	57%	8
Cooper	33%	2	Lane	15%	5
Wilkins	30%	2	Wilson	67%	3
London	63%	3	Schlenker	58%	2
Lorank	55%	9	Campbell	55%	2

Exhibit 10.3 Data for Customer Profitability Map example.

The actual Customer Profitability Map (the plot of each of these customers) has already been done, and you've seen it. This is the data set that created the Customer Profitability Map you saw earlier in this chapter.

Using this Customer Profitability Map, let's get "down and dirty" and do a thorough CPM analysis.

Total Quadrant Weighting

You will recall (or at least you should recall) that Total Quadrant Weighting is simply the proportion of your total customers who fall into each of the four quadrants. In this case, the Total Quadrant Weighting is shown in Exhibit 10.4.

Hidden Liability 17%	**Target More** 22%
Avoid! 35%	**Cross-Sell** 26%

Exhibit 10.4 CPM Total Quadrant Weighting.

Please note that even though you have only taken the first step in the CPM analysis, you've already got some very powerful, interesting and useful information about the business. From just this one part of the analysis, we learn the following:

1. Just over half (52%—the total of the *Hidden Liability* and *Avoid!* quadrants) of all the customers for this business have low Resonance Scores.

   Experience shows that customers with low Resonance Scores consume a lot more than their proportionate share of time and resources. In other words, the 52% of customers who have low Resonance Scores consume much more than 52% of the business's capacity. Therefore, we can see that a lot of time and effort is being sucked up by customers who don't click well with the business.

2. Over one-third of all the customers of the business fall into the *Avoid!* quadrant. They have low Resonance Scores, which means that dealing with them is difficult and they don't really respect the business owner and the team. And then, to add insult to injury, these people are also among the least profitable of all the customers.

It's no exaggeration at all to say that this business would most likely be better off if it got rid of these customers. Valuable resources would be almost instantly freed up, and time and attention could be focused on cross-selling and attracting new customers who would be a better fit.

Following the same logic as in the first point, the customers in this quadrant suck up way more than one-third of the available resources. And they give nothing but pain and low profit in return.

In case I'm not being clear enough, let me say it another way . . .

Get rid of these people!

3. Less than a quarter of all customers fall into the *Target More* quadrant.

This fact is actually quite shocking when you think about it. It means fewer than one out of four customers are *both* great to deal with (high Resonance Score) and highly profitable for the business.

Said another way, this means that more than 75% of this business's customers are NOT the best ones for it. Talk about a tragedy!

4. Slightly more than a quarter of all the customers are great to deal with (high Resonance Score), but are in the bottom half of profitability, which puts them in the *Cross-Sell* quadrant

This means that roughly one out of four of this business's customers are like uncut diamonds. They are potentially valuable if the right actions are taken to polish them and transform them into true gems.

This represents an absolutely HUGE opportunity to build quick cash flow and profits to sustain change efforts!

Profit at Risk

Now let's take a look at how much profit could potentially evaporate if this business were to face a new, aggressive competitor, or even a vigorous competitive attack from an existing competitor.

The CPM shows us that 17% of all this business's customers fall into the *Hidden Liability* quadrant. That number, by itself, doesn't tell us anything about the Profit At Risk number, but it will in a moment.

You don't see it here, but actual customer data showed that the gross profit from customers in this quadrant for the last year totaled $46,900 (this isn't given in the data set, but you could get it from the accounting records for the business). Of course, when you do your own analysis, you will have this information ready to go.

Since each customer in this quadrant has a low Resonance Score, their relationship with the business is always tenuous. Customers with low Resonance Scores are the most likely to switch to another company if given an opportunity and encouragement. Most often the motivation for this transfer of allegiance comes from the appearance of a new competitor, or a strategic change made by an existing competitor.

In the case of customers in the *Avoid!* quadrant, their exits wouldn't really hurt the business that much. After all, these customers don't yield much of a profit.

But there is a huge potential loss (almost $47,000) if customers in the *Hidden Liability* quadrant leave. The fact that they are highly profitable for the business means that losing them, while perhaps emotionally satisfying (due to their low Resonance Scores), would be damaging in the short term.

Cross-Sell Potential

This part of the analysis looks at how much profit the business stands to gain by moving customers in the *Cross-Sell* quadrant to the mid-point profitability of the customers in your *Target More* quadrant.

After all, your *Cross-Sell* quadrant customers have high Resonance Scores. You enjoy them, get along well with them, and they most likely value and respect your business and your team.

They are worth keeping.

Because of that, it's definitely worth trying to increase the level of profitability they deliver to the business.

This analysis involves a few simple steps:

1. Determine the average profit for customers in this quadrant. In the example data, the total gross profit for customers in this quadrant was $38,100 (again, this isn't shown in the data table). With a total of 12 customers in this quadrant, the average gross profit per customer in this quadrant is $3,175.

2. Determine the average profit for customers in the *Target More* quadrant. In the example, the total gross profit for all *Target More* customers is $58,700 (not shown in the data table). With a total of 10 customers in that quadrant, the average gross profit per customer is $5,870.

3. Calculate the difference between the two average values. The difference in this case is $2,695 ($5,870 − $3,175). We will call this number the Cross-Sell Spread.

4. Multiply the Cross-Sell Spread by the total number of customers in the *Cross-Sell* quadrant. In this case, multiplying the 12 customers in the quadrant by the Cross-Sell Spread of $2,695 gives us a value of $32,340.

And there you have the Cross-Sell Potential for this business. We now know that if the business could shift the profitability of each customer in the *Cross-Sell* quadrant to the level of the average profitability for customers in the *Target More* quadrant, the business would increase its total gross profit by $32,340!!

Now of course it's not realistic to assume that every single *Cross-Sell* customer could be moved to that level (although I'd sincerely argue that they should be). But even if the business achieves only 50% of that potential, that's still more than $16,000 of additional Gross Profit that could be realized. And that would represent an amazing 42% increase over the current profitability of those same customers!

Profit Replacement Potential

This element of your analysis is similar to the Cross-Sell Potential we just covered.

The idea behind this measure is that any customers in the *Avoid!* quadrant really need to be fired. They contribute little net profit to your business, and they have low Resonance Scores. To put it plain and simple, customers in the *Avoid!* quadrant just aren't worth the effort required to have them around.

Just consider all the time these customers take from you and your team. It's common for customers in the *Avoid!* quadrant to be the largest consumers of the one resource you can never get more of—time.

These people tend to be the ones who are always nagging about small things. They're often the ones who demand immediate action, even when their timeline just isn't feasible. And *then* they have the nerve to be the ones most likely to make comments or complain about being charged too much.

In addition to consuming large amounts of time, these customers suck an awful lot of emotional energy out of you and your team. Because they have low Resonance Scores, you'll have a difficult time dealing with them. Their relationship with your business is strained, and it feels like work.

Because it is.

These customers just don't click with you, your team, and your business.

So imagine if a business could get rid of *all* the customers in the *Avoid!* quadrant. Think about how much time and emotional energy would be freed by not having to waste it on dealing with these people's demands.

What would you do with all that freed-up time and emotional energy?

If you're like most business owners, you'd make sure you spent a good chunk of the newly found time with your best customers (your *Target More* customers). And you could use some of that time to carefully target and pursue new customers who would fit into your Target More quadrant.

So here's how to do the calculation of the Profit Replacement measure:

1. Determine the average net profit for customers in the *Avoid!* quadrant. In this example, the total Gross Profit of customers in this quadrant was $47,900 (again, the amount is not shown in the data table—it comes from the business's accounting records). With a total of 16 customers in the quadrant, the average gross profit for the *Avoid!* quadrant is $2,994.

2. Determine the average net profit provided for customers in the *Target More* quadrant. In our example, the total profit for the quadrant was $58,700 (not shown in data table), with 10 customers, for an average profit of $5,870.

3. Calculate the quadrant-spread between these two numbers. In this case, the spread is $2,876 ($5,870 – $2,994).

4. Estimate how much time, on average, is spent on a typical customer from the *Avoid!* quadrant. This is a subjective guess in many cases, but do your best. In our example, the owner estimated that a typical *Avoid!* customer consumed 35 hours over the course of a year.

5. Estimate how much time, on average, is spent on a typical customer from the *Target More* quadrant. In this example, the business owner figured it was about 12 hours a year.

6. Divide the time estimate for the typical *Avoid!* customer by the time estimate for a typical *Target More* customers. In this case, the resulting value is 2.9 (35 hours / 12 hours).

   This is the theoretical number of new *Target More* customers that could be served for every single customer from the *Avoid!* quadrant who is convinced to take his/her business elsewhere.

However, it's very unlikely that the entire time freed up by firing *Avoid!* customers would be spent on new *Target More* customers. Most likely, a portion of the newfound time and resources would be spent on other projects, and improving relationships with existing customers in other quadrants.

Because of that fact, pick some percentage of the freed time that could realistically be spent attracting and working with new *Target More* customers. In the example, the business owner used 50% (they felt half of the newly free time would be spent on new *Target More* customers).

7. Now multiply the quadrant-spread from Step 3 by the time multiplier from Step 6, and multiply the resulting number by the percentage estimated in Step 7. Then multiply the value obtained by the number of total customers in the *Avoid!* quadrant.

    In the example, the step would give a result of $66,723 ($2,876 × 2.9 × 50% × 16 = $66,723!)

So what does this number mean?

In our example, the Profit Replacement Potential measure shows that if the business owner fired all 16 of the customers in the *Avoid!* quadrant, and devoted 50% of the newly freed time to serving new customers in the *Target More* quadrant, total Gross Profit would shoot up by a whopping $66,723.

Another way of looking at this information is to think about what each of those *Avoid!* customers is costing the business. And yes, they are costing the business, because until they are fired, they will continue to suck up time and emotional energy but will return little net profit.

So if the Profit Replacement Potential analysis shows that the business would be better off by almost $67,000 if it fired its *Avoid!* customers, and if the current *Avoid!* customers are creating a scarcity of resources and capacity, then each customer in the *Avoid!*

quadrant is currently COSTING the business $4,187 ($67,000 / 16) in lost profit potential!

Enough said?

Get rid of them.

NOW!

ROLL UP YOUR SLEEVES

Now it's time for you to get down and dirty. You are going to dig deep into your business and accounting records to ferret out the information you need to do your very own Customer Profitability Map and CPM Analysis.

I've provided you with some worksheets to guide you in your work, but I can't provide you with the actual labor (well, actually I can—that's part of what most of my consulting engagements entail). But for now, you need to do it yourself. Of course, you can obtain a lot of this information from your team, if they usually help you with that kind of thing.

You will find a blank worksheet as Exhibit 10.5. Carefully list each customer your business has, or each customer it has dealt with over the last year if your list of "lifetime customers" is too long.

On the worksheet, you have room to record the sales, cost of sales, Gross Profit, and Resonance Score for each customer. Take the time to plot the data you gather on a grid to create your own Customer Profitability Map. Then revisit the section earlier in this chapter and calculate the following for your business:

- Total quadrant weighting

- Profit at risk

- Cross-sell potential

- Profit replacement potential

You can also visit the Found Money section of my Web site, www.stevewilkinghoff.com. There you can download additional worksheets, as well as work with an interactive tool to streamline your Customer Profitability Map efforts.

Customer	(A) Sales	(B) Cost of Sales	(C) Gross Profit (B − A)	(D) Profitability (C / A)	Resonance Score

Exhibit 10.5 Customer Profitability Map worksheet.

CHAPTER

11

FOUND MONEY MATH
(It's Fun—Really)

In this chapter, we're going to cover several key topics. Although these topics are different, they are all connected by what I call the Found Money Math. Each topic shows how one or more of the components of the Found Money system combines with all the other elements of the system to create the financial results you desire from your business so it serves your dream lifestyle.

But first, a quick story about how a business almost marketed itself to death.

There is an ultra-common but oh-so-dangerous trap that beguiles unsuspecting business owners every single day. Creating a business that serves your dream lifestyle demands that you be aware of this trap and that you remain constantly on guard to not fall into it.

The trap is something I call Marketing Blindness.

Marketing Blindness is the situation in which a business owner falls under the spell of a particular marketing concept, tactic, or strategy. The owner becomes mesmerized and seduced by it. He or she is practically hypnotized into focusing on that particular tactic and blindly relying on it. And in the process, the owner fervently hopes that it will somehow provide the results he or she wants.

A business owner afflicted with Marketing Blindness almost always displays symptoms of an additional marketing malady that usually goes along with it. I call this other marketing malady Volumitis.

Volumitis is the burning belief that the key to a successful (and profitable) business lies in growing revenue, getting more business, making more sales, and attracting as many customers as possible. The victims of Volumitis get excited about growing their customer bases and increasing revenue, as if that was the answer to all their problems.

Marketing Blindness and Volumitis are *very* dangerous business diseases. And yes, they are diseases. They cause any business (and its owner) to become sick and weak. And like human diseases, if they are not detected early and quickly eradicated, they can do serious damage and even cause business death.

Uncorrected, Marketing Blindness and Volumitis can be fatal.

RUSSIAN ROULETTE FOR YOUR BUSINESS

Marketing Blindness and Volumitis, and the desire they create in their victims for continually getting more business, bring to mind the concept of Russian Roulette.

Actually, it's worse than playing Russian Roulette. It's like playing Russian Roulette over and over and over and over again. It's a foregone conclusion that the "game" is going to continue until it ends in disaster. It's only a matter of *when*, not *if*, it will end. And it doesn't take all that long before the person playing the game is hurt.

Here's an example. Consider the following business owners, who demonstrate a classic case of this disease. The business owners (let's call them Mary and Tom) have seen their net profit continually decrease over the last several years. They are both absolutely baffled by this situation, because the business has been busier and busier each year.

Mary and Tom have been running full-tilt, at a completely unsustainable pace, just to keep up. They are absolutely exhausted, tired of working so hard, burning out, and just so frustrated. Actually, they are more than frustrated; Mary and Tom are angry. Even though they are so busy and work so hard, they are continually tight on cash and just can't seem to get ahead.

They are so angry, frustrated, and fed up that they are ready to quit.

Their industry has seen a couple of large competitors (big box stores) move into their market in the last five years. Mary and Tom complain that those competitors have forced market prices lower. And they say that makes it harder and harder for them to compete.

So far, though, Tom and Mary have resisted the urge to get out of the business because they took on debt over the previous years as their business suffered, and they don't think they will get enough to cover the debt if they sell. The business they have built simply doesn't have any value the way it's been created and run for years.

Despite Mary and Tom's problems, they really do love their business. And if they can help it, they sure don't want to stop.

Their summarized operations for the three most recent years are shown in Exhibit 11.1.

Mary and Tom are fictitious, but their story is based on a real-life situation. The numbers have also been changed. But here's what happened when we met and discussed their future.

During our initial meeting, I asked a lot of tough and penetrating questions. That was an uncomfortable experience for them, because I wouldn't let them make easy excuses or statements based on information they weren't really sure about. Deep down, in their gut, they really did know a lot of the answers to the tough questions.

	Three Years Ago	Two Years Ago	Last Year
Sales	$175,000	$195,000	$210,000
Gross Profit (%)	66,500 (38%)	68,250 (35%)	58,800 (28%)
Expenses	40,000	42,000	39,000
Net Profit	26,500	26,250	19,800

Exhibit 11.1 Summary of Mary and Tom's business.

They were just reluctant to actually face the truth.

Eventually, Tom and Mary confronted the truth. And that's when things really started to happen.

They told me how they had developed a very successful marketing approach to counteract the large competitors when they moved into their market. They bragged about how no one else in their market was creative enough to try it. And they proudly pointed to the increased revenue they had seen since they implemented the new tactic.

But the conversation always looped back to how frustrated they were because they were always trapped, working in the business. There never seemed to be enough money or time to break free of the business.

They also talked about how, despite their troubles, they felt lucky to have created their new marketing tactic. They went on to say that, given how difficult and challenging it was, they couldn't imagine the difficulties they'd be facing if they hadn't implemented that tactic.

I have to take a moment here to say that I always find it quite amusing when a business owner is so quick to blame price competition for their problems. I guess it's human nature to try to blame someone, or something else, rather than looking inward. In the majority of cases, while price competition is a factor, it's not the underlying cause of most problems.

Anyway, I wasn't convinced that their problems were entirely due to the price pressures in their market (though they were absolutely positive that was the source of their suffering).

In fact, I had a very strong hunch that competitive price pressures were not the problem at all.

Our first meeting ended like so many of my sessions do. I packed up my laptop and my notes, and gave them a list of homework activities to do. Their homework was to gather certain information from their records so we could start working together to improve their business and their lives.

It's a fact of life that you can't do a good job of effectively moving someplace new and better (i.e., toward your dream lifestyle) unless you first can figure out exactly where you're starting from.

To help move Tom and Mary someplace new, I asked them to go through their last three years and pull a sample of their actual sales invoices.

We already knew that their sales revenue had been increasing, but I wanted to find out what was actually happening to the underlying volume of activity.

It took a lot of work on their part.

It usually does. You see, most business owners don't realize the power of the data that flows through their business on a daily basis. And because of that, they never set up an effective system to capture and track that information. That means they have to go hunting through old records to extract the information necessary to find their hidden profit and cash flow, and thereby improve and serve their dream lifestyle.

Tom and Mary kept working on getting the information for me. And they kept complaining that it was too much work. And I kept nagging them to keep at it. Finally they came up with the information we needed, as shown in Exhibit 11.2.

	Three Years Ago	Two Years Ago	Last Year
Total Revenue	$175,000	$195,000	$210,000
Number of Sales	1,000	1,150	1,350
Average Sale	$175	$170	$156

Exhibit 11.2 Data obtained by Mary and Tom.

It was clear from this information why they were feeling busier than ever. They actually *were* busier than ever. They were busier than ever because the physical volume of their transactions had increased by 35% in two years.

In other words, *they* were doing 35% more work in their business. An increase of 35% in volume would be enough to challenge even the best managed and best capitalized business. But Mary and Tom's situation was made worse by the fact that despite having 35% more *sales activity*, their actual *sales revenue* only grew by 20%.

A quick bit of math showed that the size of each transaction had decreased by 11%. To determine that, I simply divided the total revenue by the number of sales to get the average sale for each period.

But while the average transaction decreased by 11%, their direct costs remained essentially flat. This explained the decrease in Gross Profit their business suffered (from $66,500 down to $58,800).

To summarize, the data from their business showed they were doing more and more transactions, yet making less and less on each one.

When pressed, Mary and Tom admitted that their "surefire marketing tactic" that no one else was doing was to stop adding a delivery charge on each of their sales (free delivery). Of course, they still had to shoulder the costs of delivering the order (just as they always had). This was the equivalent of making a price reduction (you'll read more about how bad price reductions can be in the next chapter).

Naturally, their customers loved it, and the volume of activity went up. But each transaction actually created less Gross Profit than before the new marketing tactic (when they used to charge for delivery).

Mary and Tom told me that the idea was suggested by an advertising salesperson. That salesperson assured them that a catchy gimmick like that, in the salesperson's opinion, would definitely drive sales higher.

The salesperson was absolutely right! Sales had indeed increased. In fact, sales and revenue had climbed to record levels.

But so what?

While sales were climbing to record levels, profits were also reaching record levels ... record *lows*, that is.

And record lows in profit are definitely *not* records you can be proud of.

However, this story has a happy ending. We got to the business and the owners in time to save them.

We worked with the owners to determine what margin the business needed to create to be a success for its owners. We used the Customer Profitability Map to figure out which customers would be the best ones to create that margin. Then we created specific tactics and measures to go out and get those customers.

THE GROSS PROFIT FORMULA, REVISITED

Earlier in this book, you learned that Gross Profit is calculated by subtracting the cost of sales from sales revenue for all products and services sold.

That's the traditional way of defining it.

But there's another formula for Gross Profit that is much more helpful for maximizing the profit, cash flow, fun, and free time you get from your business. And now that you understand the basics of Gross Margin and Gross Profit, it's time to learn this advanced formula and start harnessing its power.

Since this "advanced" way of looking at Gross Profit is part of the Found Money system, I have summoned every single ounce of my creative energy and called it ... the Found Money Gross Profit Formula.

Okay, so maybe it's not all that creative. I can admit it. But it's still a great name, because it differentiates this way of looking at Gross Profit from the traditional "accounting definition."

Defining Gross Profit the Found Money way allows you to see how you can harness the power of your Found Money tools and knowledge.

Get ready. Here's the Found Money Gross Profit formula:

Found Money Gross Profit = customers × frequency × customer Gross Margin

This formula doesn't really look all that special, I'll admit. In fact, there are variations of it in almost every area of business writing. But that doesn't mean it isn't incredibly useful. It is. And in just a few moments you will see just how powerful it can be.

For now, though, let's make sure you clearly understand what the formula is saying.

It says that the Gross Profit for your business depends directly on how many customers your business has, how often those customers buy from your business, and how much Gross Margin each of those transactions generates for your business.

The Gross Profit of any business is the "engine" that drives a satisfactory net profit, which in turn allows it to serve its owners' dream lifestyle. In other words, the degree to which your business serves your dream lifestyle depends directly on the combination of those three elements.

THE FOUND MONEY GROSS PROFIT FORMULA IN ACTION

Let's look an example of two different businesses to clarify this concept. Some relevant data from each of the businesses is shown in Exhibit 11.3.

	Business Alpha	Business Beta
(A) Number of Customers	1,000	370
(B) Frequency per Year	0.5	6.0
(C) Average Gross Margin	$ 350	$ 79
Gross Profit (A × B × C)	$175,000	$175,380

Exhibit 11.3 A comparison of two different businesses.

From the data, it's obvious we are looking at two businesses with completely different approaches and structures. Business Alpha maintains a large number of customers who only buy something about every two years, but they are purchasing fairly big-ticket items when they do buy. Business Beta has far fewer customers (about one-third as many), but they buy a smaller ticket item much more frequently (about every two months).

But look at the end result. Both businesses have pretty much identical Gross Profit results. Each business has about $175,000 to cover overhead expenses, fund additional growth, and sustain the owner's dream lifestyle.

THE WIZARD OF (PROFIT) OZ

The above example leads nicely into a discussion about how to apply the Found Money Gross Profit formula to maximize the profit, cash flow, fun, and free-time you get out of your business.

Another quick look at the formula tells you that there are really three (well, maybe four) ways to create more gross profit for your business:

1. Get more customers

2. Sell them something more often

3. Increase the average gross margin of each transaction

4. A combination of any of the above

Admittedly, this concept is nothing new. It's been around in several forms, and has been written about by hundreds of people over a lot of years. But despite that, it seems like the concept too often gets forgotten in the frantic activity that goes on "in the trenches" day-to-day in business. The truth remains that any effort, tactics, or strategies you create and deploy that do one of those four things is sure to increase your total Gross Profit.

The key thing to realize is that maximizing your profit and cash flow depends on leveraging your business resources to the hilt. Each business has a limit on its resources. There's only so much time, energy, and commitment you and your team can muster.

After all, your goal is to build a business that provides the dream lifestyle you desire and to maximize your profit and cash flow. And I'm willing to bet that your dream lifestyle doesn't include spending every spare moment of your time and every spare ounce of energy you've got trying to work harder and harder (like an increasingly fast treadmill).

I'm willing to bet that unless you are a true workaholic, your dream lifestyle involves just the opposite. It probably involves you having the time, money, and relaxed mental state to pursue whatever "non-business" interests you'd like. Fulfilling your dream lifestyle through your business *demands* that you focus on the part of the formula that gives you the most leverage.

Makes complete sense, doesn't it?

So given that, let's explore the three main ways to increase your profit (we will ignore the fourth method because it is simply a blend of two or more of the first three).

Get More Customers

Getting more customers is usually the first (and often the only) way many business owners (and even a lot of their advisors, such as accountants, marketers, and consultants) rely on to try to increase their profit and improve their dream lifestyle.

They think they should crank up their advertising efforts, or maybe offer some special sale and really "promote it hard" (which by the way, is a really bad move in most situations—visit the Found Money section of my Web site, www.stevewilkinghoff.com for an explanation).

Most media salespeople really encourage this method of increasing profits. The advertising reps for television stations, radio stations, newspapers, and Yellow Pages seem to try to tap into this angle as their default. They talk about how well their audience demographics match up with your business. They talk about how a great ad (usually created by their creative department) will get a bunch of people through your doors. They paint a wonderful picture of a booming business, filled with customers, if you'll just advertise with THEM.

And while there's not necessarily anything wrong with that approach, remember this. The media sales rep gets paid when they sell you advertising. They don't get paid to make you more money.

But YOU get paid when your business makes a profit. Don't forget that. Ever!

This "Get More Customers" method of increasing money has several problems.

First of all, getting more customers means (sooner or later) you will need to increase your business infrastructure and overhead. As more and more customers walk in to your business, you will need to hire more team members, invest in more inventory, and carry a higher investment in accounts receivable.

Over time, you might need to increase your overhead in other ways too. Perhaps you will need to rent larger space, buy more desks and computers, add more service vehicles, and so on.

So this method of profit growth is an expensive one.

The second problem with this approach is that it comes with a built-in limit. Remember that to have your business make money, you need to make sure your Return on Investment doesn't slide as you grow your net profit (recall the Triple Overlap).

To maintain a Triple Overlap, you must carefully manage your growth in new customers. That means this method of increasing your profit is limited to the rate of growth permitted by your ROI and cash flow.

The third problem is that there isn't any way to leverage the "Get More Customers" growth tactic. It traps you and your business in a linear growth mode that forces you to work harder to make more money.

Take a look at the chart in Exhibit 11.4, which demonstrates what I mean. It shows how much your overall Gross Profit will increase for a given increase in sales volume, given your current Gross Margin.

		Sales Volume Increase (%)						
		5%	**10%**	**15%**	**20%**	**25%**	**30%**	**35%**
	20%	5%	10%	15%	20%	25%	30%	35%
	25%	5%	10%	15%	20%	25%	30%	35%
	30%	5%	10%	15%	20%	25%	30%	35%
	35%	5%	10%	15%	20%	25%	30%	35%
Current Gross	**40%**	5%	10%	15%	20%	25%	30%	35%
Margin (%)	**45%**	5%	10%	15%	20%	25%	30%	35%
	50%	5%	10%	15%	20%	25%	30%	35%
	55%	5%	10%	15%	20%	25%	30%	35%
	60%	5%	10%	15%	20%	25%	30%	35%

Exhibit 11.4 Gross Profit increase from customer volume increase.

Is this very exciting?

Not in my opinion. It's simply a case of buying yourself a higher-paying job. And while there's nothing wrong with making more money, this approach forces a linear trade-off. Work 15% harder in your business and you make 15% more money.

In other words, if you work hard, market effectively and increase the number of customers you get, the best you can do is to increase your Gross Profit by the same percentage as you increase your sales volume. If you increase the number of customers you have by 10%, your total Gross Profit will increase by 10%.

Exhibit 11.5 is an example using some actual numbers.

	Before	After
(A) Number of Customers	1,000	1,100
Increase	10%	
(B) Frequency	0.5	0.5
(C) Average Gross Profit	$ 350	$ 350
Gross Profit (A × B × C)	$175,000	$192,500
Increase	10%	

Exhibit 11.5 Impact of 10% customer volume increase.

It's clear that it is only possible to make as much additional profit as you and your team have the ability (or willingness) to work harder and longer. That's a painful way to grow profit, and it's one that is completely at odds with your effort to maximize the profit, cash flow, fun, and free time you get from your business (and live your dream lifestyle)

You can only expect your business to work as hard as you do when you rely on this tactic.

Sell to Existing Customers More Often (Increase Frequency)

Another way to increase your total net profit using the Found Money Formula is to increase how often your existing customers buy from you (the frequency of their purchases).

Sadly, this tactic is often completely ignored by business owners.

That has always puzzled me.

After all, your business already has a relationship with your existing customers. Even more importantly, you know who they are. Compare that to trying to get new customers who you don't even know yet.

And it's very inexpensive to reach out and communicate with your existing customers. Paradoxically it's very expensive to try to attract new customers that you don't even know yet.

Oh yeah, and because you know who your existing customers are, you can pinpoint where they fit into your Customer

Profitability Map. That gives you the absolute luxury of deciding whether you should be encouraging them to buy more from you, whether you want to encourage them to buy more often, and even whether you should be spending any time and effort dealing with them at all.

But despite all these advantages, I'm continually shocked by how seldom this tactic is used.

For example, I was recently talking to a friend of mine, who is also a business owner. He was telling me how expensive his business had become. He talked about how much money he spent each year on advertising for his business, and yet just seemed to manage to maintain the same profit each year.

He said he never seemed to be able to find the right advertising to increase his profits.

I asked him what the frequency of his existing customers was. You could have heard a pin drop in his store. He looked at me with a very blank look. He finally broke the silence when he said he didn't really know.

But to his credit, he *admitted* that he didn't know. And when we talked about it some more, he realized he could at least start with an estimate.

We went to his computer and quickly went through his customer list for the previous year. Customer record after customer record, he made the comment that "he (or she) doesn't really come in here much anymore."

When I asked him why that was, his answer (again giving full credit for honesty) was that he didn't know.

When I asked him when the last time he specifically invited those same "old" customers to the store it was silent again.

And guess what? I'm willing to bet that if I had been in *your* business that day, and had asked *you* those questions, *your* answers would have been the same.

That's how it seems to be with most business owners. They seem to have this weird desire to spend more time and money trying to attract new customers, at the same time that they practically ignore (or forget about) working with their existing customers to increase the frequency of their visits and purchases.

Yet increasing the frequency of existing customers is a *much* easier way to increase total Gross Profit. And it's much cheaper too. After all, it's way, way easier to contact people you already know (your existing customers) than trying to reach out, attract and capture new customers. You already know who your existing customers are, where they live, and how to contact them via mail, phone, or e-mail.

So it makes sense that trying to increase frequency should be the preferred tactic over trying to attract new customers. Doesn't it?

But despite being logical and making good sense, it sadly doesn't seem to be the tactic most business owners turn to first.

Despite the fact that increasing frequency is a more effective and cheaper way to grow gross profit, it still has a major drawback. The relationship between increasing frequency and increased profits is still a linear one.

Take a look at the chart in Exhibit 11.6. It shows the impact a change in frequency of purchase can have on a business.

		Frequency Increase (%)						
		5%	10%	15%	20%	25%	30%	35%
	20%	5%	10%	15%	20%	25%	30%	35%
	25%	5%	10%	15%	20%	25%	30%	35%
	30%	5%	10%	15%	20%	25%	30%	35%
	35%	5%	10%	15%	20%	25%	30%	35%
Current Gross	40%	5%	10%	15%	20%	25%	30%	35%
Margin (%)	45%	5%	10%	15%	20%	25%	30%	35%
	50%	5%	10%	15%	20%	25%	30%	35%
	55%	5%	10%	15%	20%	25%	30%	35%
	60%	5%	10%	15%	20%	25%	30%	35%

Exhibit 11.6 Gross Profit increase from customer frequency increase.

I'm still not all that impressed. Even though it's easier (and cheaper) to increase frequency than to increase your number of customers, this tactic still suffers from the linearity problem. Again, your business will only be able to work as hard as you and your team do (and are willing and able to). But because it's generally cheaper to increase frequency than it is to find new customers this tactic is preferable to the "get more customers" tactic.

Increase the Average Gross Profit of a Transaction

This element of the Found Money Formula is almost always ignored by business owners. Paradoxically, this method of increasing Gross Profit is the absolute *best* way to do it.

This method alone can *explode* the money your business creates for you. And it's the key to creating a business that serves your dream lifestyle.

This tactic involves either increasing your prices, or selling additional items with each sale (known as cross-selling or up-selling), or both.

Increasing prices will be dealt with in depth in the next chapter (because it is a large and important topic on its own). For the time being, we will confine our discussion to selling additional items.

Almost every business offers more than one particular product or service. In most cases your customers could really benefit by buying and using at least some of the additional products and services your business could provide.

But most businesses don't actively and systematically discuss additional products and services with their customers. That's a sad fact that should be considered a crime (a crime against your dream lifestyle), because it robs the business of so much money.

The next section, "It's All About Leverage," discusses the four ways that Gross Margin and Gross Profit can be increased.

But before we look at that, though, here's an example from my experience as a partner of a large accounting firm. Time and time again, the "old" partners of the firm would say things like, "our clients wouldn't buy that," or "client A wouldn't want to pay for something like that."

Now you need to know those kinds of things were usually said when someone would make an "out-of-the-box" suggestion (from the point of view of a traditional accounting firm). Even though this large firm was fairly progressive (as accounting firms go), it still had a pretty small "box," so it wasn't difficult to be out of it.

What always blew me away was that the very clients who "would never want that," according to the old-school partners, very often *did* want it. In fact, the clients wanted those other things so much that they often went and bought them from someone else.

Those clients could have bought those same extra services from the partners of my firm—if they had only been asked. The result was lost revenue and profit for the firm, and a weakened relationship with the client.

My experiences with the old-school partners are, sadly, very, very common in all businesses, not just accounting firms. Thinking about and offering additional services to existing customers just doesn't seem to make it onto the radar of most business owners.

After all, you and your team know all the different products and services your business can provide. But that knowledge is actually a liability when it comes to offering them to your customers.

Because you are so familiar with the wide range of products and services your business *could* deliver, you tend to take them for granted. The trap is that because *you* know about all of them, you assume your customers know about them too. And that causes you to assume your customers know what they want from your business.

But your customers *don't* know.

So ask your customers what they are really trying to accomplish with their purchases. Then firmly suggest things you honestly believe will be things they need and will benefit from. Tell them about *all* the things your business can provide for them and do for them.

What's the benefit of doing that?

Well for one, your customers will be impressed that you're thinking about them. Even if they don't want what you're suggesting, they will still recognize that you, your team, and your business are proactively trying to make their lives better. And that will only deepen your relationship with your customers (i.e., increase Resonance Scores).

A second benefit is that your customers will very often be delighted to find out about some of those other things. And they will become customers with a higher average Gross Profit (and much higher Resonance Score).

IT'S ALL ABOUT LEVERAGE

Now you realize how incredibly powerful the Found Money Formula can be, and how it can be used to drive your business to the point where it serves you and provides you with your dream lifestyle—the one you and your family members crave and deserve.

But how do you decide where to focus most of your efforts?

After all, it might not be possible to increase all 3 elements of the formula by the same amount (in fact it's never really as easy and simple as in our example).

Some businesses might have no problem increasing prices (don't shudder, we will talk more about prices in Chapter 12, Pricing Bootcamp) by large amounts each year. Other businesses have a very easy time finding new customers (of course, they should always be the right type of customer according to the Customer Profitability Map for that business). And still other businesses have a relatively easy time increasing the frequency of customer purchases.

To help you decide where to focus your limited resources (time, energy, and money), you can run a whole bunch of trial and error scenarios. You can also use the Found Money software to perform these types of scenarios. You can also visit the Found Money section of my Web site www.stevewilkinghoff.com to find some useful tools to help you figure out where to focus.

There are some guidelines, though, that apply to the vast majority of businesses. So as a starting point, here are some general guidelines:

- The quickest way to raise total Gross Profit in any business is to increase prices (more about this topic in the Chapter 12).

- The next best method to increase Gross Profit is to cross-sell by systematically offering and educating customers about the other products and services your business sells during the existing sales process.

- The next best method is to increase the frequency of customer purchases.

- The final way to increase total Gross Profit should be trying to attract new customers (but this is where most business owners seem to want to start).

This hierarchy is so effective, yet so misunderstood, that it warrants some specific comments about each element.

Increase Prices

This is so important to the overall success of your business and to transforming your business into a vehicle to create your dream lifestyle, that it gets its own chapter (Chapter 12, Your Pricing Bootcamp).

But as a preview, consider the table in Exhibit 11.7.

		Price Increase (%)						
		5%	10%	15%	20%	25%	30%	35%
	20%	25%	50%	75%	100%	125%	150%	175%
	25%	20%	40%	60%	80%	100%	120%	140%
	30%	17%	33%	50%	67%	83%	100%	117%
	35%	14%	29%	43%	57%	71%	86%	100%
Current Gross	40%	13%	25%	38%	50%	63%	75%	88%
Margin (%)	45%	11%	22%	33%	44%	56%	67%	78%
	50%	10%	20%	30%	40%	50%	60%	70%
	55%	9%	18%	27%	36%	45%	55%	64%
	60%	8%	17%	25%	33%	42%	50%	58%

Exhibit 11.7 Gross Profit increase from price increase.

This table excites me! And it should excite you, too.

This chart shows that focusing your efforts on increasing prices creates a huge multiplier effect. The table describes the percentage increase a business will realize, given a combination of price increase and Gross Margin. For example, look down the column for a 5% increase in price, until you get to the last row (for a 60% gross margin).

The effect here is the lowest for the entire table. But even so, it's still 8%. That means that, given that combination of price increase and gross margin, a 5% price increase would still create a multiplier effect, and increase your gross profit by 8%.

And that's the "worst" you could do. All the other effects (various combinations of price increases and gross margins) would create an even larger multiplier.

That's leverage!

Now before you get all defensive, I know what you're going to say. And yes, some customers may leave if you increase your prices. But don't worry. Just hang on tight, for now. Chapter 12 will address that very concern—and show you it's just not valid. You'll see. I promise.

Offer Other Products and Services at the Time Of Sale

This tactic is the next easiest way to lift your total Gross Profit.

Why?

Because you've already done all the really hard work. You've taken the time and committed the money and effort to create a customer, provided a place of business for them to come to, hired team members to help them, and built a relationship with them. And you've accomplished all that by filling one of their needs with one of your products or services.

The odds are really, really high that the customer who is standing at the cash register at any particular time also has other needs that your business could fill. But the odds are just as high that your particular customer isn't thinking about those other needs right now (and therefore isn't looking for a solution at the moment), or doesn't know your business can offer them. But because you are already dealing with a person who knows you and your business, if you *do* offer additional products and services, the impact is almost immediate. At the very least, the effect is much more immediate than trying to market for new customers.

The classic example of this is when you go out to a nice restaurant. After you have eaten your meal your server comes by with that impressive dessert tray. Now, admit it: You're already full and probably weren't about to ask to see what they had for dessert, were you?

But because the server brings the dessert tray by your table to show it off, someone in your group will likely end up buying something.

And bang!

The restaurant has just used this classic technique to increase their total Gross Profit (guess where the restaurant has a higher Gross Margin—the meal, or the dessert?).

And you can do the same thing in your business.

Increase Frequency of Purchases

This is your third-best tactic in the hierarchy.

It is not as effective at increasing total Gross Profit as a price increase, and it's not as immediate as offering additional products and services to a customer who is already buying something.

But it's a lot better than trying to find a new customer.

It's better than trying to find a new customer because, like offering additional products at the time of sale, this tactic harnesses the power of established relationships you have with existing customers. And these people already know you, your team, your business, and the products and services you deliver (or at least some of your products and services).

You've already managed to break through all the marketing noise people are forced to endure every day. You've got an established relationship with these people.

And these two facts mean you can reach out and communicate with them easily and cheaply. You already know who they are, where they live, how to reach them via phone, mail, and e-mail (you *do* capture that information, don't you?) and what they've bought from you in the past.

And because you've already got experience dealing with these people, you know exactly where they fall on your Customer Profitability Map. That means you've got the luxury of looking at all these people and deciding whether you really do want them to come back more often (or not, in the case of customers with low Resonance Scores).

While increasing the frequency of purchase is simple and easy, that advantage sometimes seems to be its downfall. Many business owners miss out on using the power of this technique because they are looking for something harder. I don't know why this is, but an awful lot of business owners and managers seem to get so busy trying to knock the door down (the hard way to do it), that they don't even bother to try the doorknob (the easy way). That just doesn't make any sense, at all, does it?

For example, I was working with a hearing aid clinic a while ago. All the team members were in the consulting session, and frequency of purchase came up. Each team member agreed that their clients needed to buy new batteries on a regular basis to keep their hearing aid working.

But they also all said that many clients never came in to buy their batteries from this hearing aid clinic. The clients ended up going to large retailers to buy them. Not because the batteries were any cheaper at the big retailers, but because the clients would ignore batteries for their hearing aid until they suddenly realized they were about to run out. Then they would head to the nearest place to buy the batteries.

So I suggested they send a letter to each client. The letter offered to keep the client's information on file. Then each month, when the client's battery supply was just about to run out (hearing aid batteries have a pretty predictable lifespan, based on the type of hearing aid), a new supply would be automatically mailed out to the client, and their credit card would be charged for the cost.

This idea was met with a lot of negativity and criticism. They all told me how it wouldn't work. Their clients wouldn't want to do that (or so they tried to tell me). After all, this was just not something that "had ever been done" before in this practice.

But I kept at it, and convinced them to try sending the letters. If we wrote it well, I argued, clients who weren't interested in the offer simply wouldn't take advantage of the service. There was no risk to the clinic, other than paying for the postage for the letters (but that was minor). Clients who didn't want this new service wouldn't be angry or offended (which was what the client was worried about).

So, for a few hundred dollars, the clinic owner mailed out a bunch of letters.

And the results were great!

The clinic owner was surprised, but very happy at how many clients jumped to take advantage of this new service. In fact, the clinic owner told me, many of their clients even commented on what a great service it was to offer. They not only took advantage of it, but they viewed it as a tremendously useful and wonderful service.

That was a huge double-win! The clinic increased the purchase frequency, and delighted its clients in the process (increased Resonance Scores).

Get More Customers

This is the last method of increasing total Gross Profit on our list. And it's the last method for a reason. It's the most expensive, most difficult, and riskiest method, and takes the longest time period to produce any results.

And yet, this is the method most business owners jump right into when they try to increase their profits. Frankly (and there's just no way to sugarcoat this) that's just plain *dumb*! It doesn't make any sense at all.

Why doesn't it make sense? There are three reasons:

1. It costs a lot of money, and despite your best efforts, it's almost impossible to make sure only people in your *Target More* quadrant receive your message.

2. It's slow, because it's usually necessary to reach potential customers many times to get your message to "stick" with

them. And then you need to wait until they need (or think they need) what you sell.

3. It's difficult. You can never be certain that your efforts at attracting new customers are effectively received by your target. Or that they are interpreted in the way you want. Or that the recipient will fully understand what it is you want them to do.

I'm not saying this method should never be used. It has a crucial role in building a business that truly serves your dream lifestyle. But you need to understand that this method must be carefully targeted to only attract the right people (those in your *Target More* quadrant) after you have done a proper Customer Profitability Map. And you must also understand that this method is the slowest to produce results and is also the most expensive method.

So this method definitely has a place in building your business and increasing Gross Profit, but it's only a small piece of the total picture. Don't fall into the common trap of thinking that this method is the key to your success. The truth is, you can dramatically move your business toward serving your dream lifestyle whether or not you use this method. So don't rely on just this one.

Unless you want to struggle and suffer like every one of your competitors, that is.

COST/VOLUME/PROFIT ANALYSIS

Okay, I'll admit that it's a really ugly and academic-sounding name (and if you're ugly, academic, or both, please don't be offended).

But get over the name! Because it's a very powerful tool that you can use to increase the profit, cash flow, and earnings from your business.

Cost/Volume/Profit Analysis (CVPA) can be used to make strategic and tactical business decisions that your competitors will practically swear are illegal. And they will swear to the alleged illegality of it because of how successful your business will suddenly become when CVPA is properly applied.

But like do-it-yourself tattooing, CVPA can be dangerous, too. To make it safe, you need to develop a thorough knowledge about it, and practice proper technique.

CVPA gives you the power to explore and test the impact of various changes in the costs and sales volumes for your business. And you can see the impact of those changes on the level of profit, fun, and free time your business gives you.

Let's jump right into an example, so you can begin to understand the power of CVPA.

Let's assume you have a business with a Gross Profit Percentage of 40%. That means your sales mix will provide a blended Gross Profit of $40 for every $100 in sales. Assume as well that the overhead for your business is $515,000 (overhead refers to all the expenses that are not direct costs—rent, utilities, advertising, management salaries, etc.).

One of the first things the CVP Analysis will do is allow you to see what total sales volume your business will need to reach its break-even point.

Break-even is the point where the Gross Profit on total sales exactly offsets the overhead required to run the business. In other words, it's the point where sales volume reaches a level that provides the business with neither a net loss, nor a net profit.

The formula looks like this:

$$\text{Breakeven Sales Volume} = \frac{\text{Total Overhead}}{\text{Gross Profit (\%)}}$$

$$= \frac{\$515,000}{40\%}$$

$$= \$1,287,500$$

Our CVPA reveals that this business must generate $1,287,500 in total sales simply to cover all the overhead.

This number is very useful at helping grow and manage a business.

Suppose, for example, that the business in our example has recently increased its overhead by a large amount (up to the $515,000) in anticipation of increased growth. That may be a great plan, but if this business has never achieved total sales volume in excess of $1 million in any previous year, then its owners and team better make sure they develop a concrete action plan to do that. Until the business reaches $1.287 million in sales revenue, it's going to lose money.

Failure to realize this and plan for it could seriously jeopardize the profitability of this business. Or maybe even threaten its long-term future.

CVPA AS YOUR BUSINESS ROADMAP

Now that you are familiar with CVPA, you are ready to harness its power to transform your business and your lifestyle. By following a three-step process, CVPA can give you the power to know where, and how, you can dramatically increase the profit your business creates.

Creating your Found Money Roadmap with CVPA is a little bit involved. So give your head a quick shake. Maybe grab a nice cold Red Bull (I prefer the sugar-free ones) from the fridge and get ready to really focus on this next section.

You will be following a three-step process in the following example. And this three-step process can be used in your own business in the same way we are going to use it here.

Suppose you have determined that your dream lifestyle requires your business to generate an additional income of $100,000 a year for you, and it also involves you working only three days each week. Suppose you also have decided that for you to only work three days a week, you're going to have to hire an excellent manager so that your business will continue to thrive while you're not there. You estimate that you will need to pay $85,000 a year for this person.

Finally, you also anticipate having to increase a few other areas of your existing operation, which is going to require you to add another $25,000 to your current overhead of $125,000 per year.

And just a few more data items for you to know—assume your business has current gross profit of 40%, has 1,000 customers with a frequency of 0.5 (they buy once every two years, on average), and an average Gross Profit per transaction of $350.

That's a lot of detail, I know. But that's exactly the information you are going to have to pull out of your business, and it's the information gathering process you absolutely *must* go through if you plan to create a business that serves you.

Now, let's use some CVPA to run through the steps of creating your Found Money Marketing Roadmap.

Calculate Your Planned Found Money Overhead

Add the planned overhead increases (your additional income requirement, the new manager, and other anticipated increases) needed to create a business that serves your dream lifestyle to your existing overhead.

This revised total overhead number is called your Found Money Overhead.

In this case, that total is as shown in Exhibit 11.8.

Extra owner compensation	$100,000
Manager required	$ 85,000
Additional overhead	$ 25,000
Existing overhead	$125,000
Total Found Money Overhead	**$335,000**

Exhibit 11.8 Example of planned Found Money Overhead calculation.

Calculate "Base" Found Money Break-Even Point

Given the current average gross profit per transaction of $350, it's an easy matter to calculate how many transactions your business would need to cover the Found Money Overhead.

The calculation works the same way as the basic breakeven calculation earlier in this chapter. The difference is that this time it is applied to the Found Money Overhead, rather than actual current overhead for the business (see Exhibit 11.9):

(A) Found Money Overhead	$335,000
(B) Average Gross Profit per Transaction	$ 350
(C) Breakeven Transactions (A/B)	958

Exhibit 11.9 Base Found Money break-even transactions.

So the "base" Found Money Break-Even is 958 transactions. This means the business will need to make 958 sales, given the current average gross profit of $350 per transaction.

And based on the current frequency of 0.5, if those 958 sales transactions are obtained through new customers, the business will need 1,916 new customers. Since the business currently only has 1,000 customers, it must go out and find 916 new ones to achieve the business owner's goals (as represented by the Found Money Break-Even). That is pretty disheartening, I will admit—almost doubling the number of customers in order to achieve the Found Money Break-Even is possibly out of reach of even the most capable business owners.

But before throwing your arms up in the air and concluding that your dream lifestyle is simply not achievable, let's take a few minutes to examine a few other scenarios.

Run Found Money Alternatives

The next step is to apply the Found Money Formula to test the three extreme limits that would still result in a Found Money break-even. This can be done by trial and error, but it will be made much easier with some of the tools and resources found in the Found Money section of my Web site www.stevewilkinghoff.com.

The way to find the three extremes is to hold two of the three factors in the Found Money Formula the same as their current values and change only the remaining factor until you achieve the Found Money Break even.

In our example, shown in Exhibit 11.10, the three extreme limits are as follows:

	Current Base	Customer Focus	Frequency Focus	Average Profit Focus
Customers	1,000	**1,916**	1,000	1,000
Frequency	0.5	0.5	**0.96**	0.5
Avg. Gross Profit	$350	$350	$350	**$670**
Total Gross Profit	$175,000	$335,300	$336,000	$335,000

Exhibit 11.10 Found Money alternative extreme limits.

GETTING THERE FROM HERE

Of course relying on only one of these three options will no doubt be very difficult. Relying on new customers alone (even though that's the approach most business owners seem to accept by default) would require the number of customers to almost double. Can you even imagine what that would do to the required level of staffing, workload, and infrastructure?

Relying only on increasing the customer frequency would prove just as problematic. Doubling the frequency is essentially the same (logistically speaking) as doubling the number of customers. It's probably just not possible. And it's going to cause the same logistical problems as doubling the number of customers.

Increasing average gross profit per transaction by 91% would require a massive price increase or massive decrease in costs. And while I'm a huge fan of price increases, it's probably just not possible to get increases that are *that* large and still have any business left.

But the situation is anything but hopeless if you carefully consider and plan out a blending of the elements over time. For example, assume that you decide you want to achieve your dream lifestyle over a three-year period. After all, it's your dream lifestyle. And that means it's probably a stretch from where you find yourself and your business right now. If it's not a big stretch, you haven't created a big-enough dream yet.

A dream that is an appropriately large stretch is one that you are not going to be able to achieve instantly. But it is possible to make relatively large gains toward that outcome in a relatively short period of time by effectively using the Found Money system.

So let's take a more balanced approach and look at one possible way your Found Money Formula could be transformed over the three-year period for your dream lifestyle plan.

What if you decided to target an increase of 7.5% in each of the three elements of your Found Money Formula for the next three years. What would happen to your total gross profit?

Take a look at Exhibit 11.11.

	Current	Year 1	Year 2	Year 3
Customers	1,000	1,075	1,156	1,242
Frequency	0.5	0.54	0.58	0.62
Average Gross Margin	$350	$376	$404	$435
Total Gross Profit	$175,000	$217,402	$270,078	$335,517

Exhibit 11.11 Combined impact of 7.5% increase in each element of the Found Money Gross Profit Formula.

And presto!! There you have it!

A simple, consistent increase of 7.5% each year in each element of your Found Money Formula creates an increase of 92% over the base case total gross profit, over a three-year period.

Even more important, that steady increase results in a Gross Profit that covers your Found Money Overhead. And remember, your Found Money Overhead was built around providing you an additional $100,000 in personal income *and* hiring a manager so you only had to work three days per week.

You're there! How totally cool is that?

Over a short three-year period, taking consistent actions (and tracking your results) to provide a 7.5% increase in each of the three elements of your Found Money Formula will create a whopping 92% increase in gross profit. And since that 92% increase provides your business with a Found Money Break-Even, that means your business will actually be able to provide you with your dream lifestyle (that you determined) within a three-year period.

Whew! That was a fairly long, but important chapter. In the next chapter we will take a close look at pricing and some surprising facts about it, and how powerful a Pricing Strategy can be for your success.

CHAPTER

12

YOUR PRICING BOOTCAMP

Ahh, pricing. The hottest, most contentious, most controversial, and usually the most misunderstood topic for business owners.

Most business owners I've met when doing seminars, speaking engagements, and consulting work invariably start talking about the pressures they face on pricing. They talk about pressure from customers for lower prices (customers can easily search for cheaper prices and make comparisons) and pressure from their competitors (both local and from around the globe).

Although there are definitely some industries and markets in which those complaints are valid, it's not usually the case. Despite hearing that complaint almost universally, my experience has shown that in most cases, those complaints are nothing but an excuse. They are excuses that hide laziness, lack of focus, confusion, and fear.

Situations where the price pressure complaint is valid are actually quite rare.

When I hear a business owner float the price pressure balloon, I'm pretty sure I know something about them. I know they are feeling frustrated, stressed out, overworked, and trapped by their business. They don't really run their business—it runs them.

The person making that comment has fallen under the mistaken (and dangerous) belief that they are forced to be a price taker. They look at price as something the market "gives" to them. They believe that their competition and their customers set their prices for them.

That belief causes the business to become marginalized in their market. The business becomes a helpless price taker, completely losing the ability to harness the true power of pricing to create the financial results they want and to serve their dream lifestyle.

You see, it's like this.

Price is one of the most powerful tools available to manage the growth and profit of your business. And it's also the least expensive and most effective way to speak to your target market (recall your Customer Profitability Map).

Here's a simple example to demonstrate the tremendous impact pricing can have.

Assume your business has 1,000 customers who buy from you once a year, and spend $500 each time. Also, assume your direct costs for each sale total $250 (your Cost of Goods Sold, or COGS). We'll assume overhead for the business totals $150,000.

Your income statement would look like this:

Revenue	$500,000
Cost of Goods Sold	(250,000)
Gross Profit	$250,000
Overhead	(150,000)
Net Profit	**$100,000**

Not a bad net income. $100,000 is certainly nothing to sneeze at.

But what would happen if you decided to increase prices by 5%?

Before we look at the result, it's important for you to realize that this 5% increase ($25 per sale) is going to directly increase the net profit for the business. That happens because any change to the price of a product or service has no affect on the actual cost of providing that product or service, or on the overhead your business carries.

Price increases are always pure profit!

After prices have been increased by 5%, the income statement would look like this:

Revenue	$525,000
Cost of Goods Sold	(250,000)
Gross Profit	$275,000
Overhead	(150,000)
Net Profit	**$125,000**

So that simple increase of 5% results in a total of $25,000 in additional profit for you and your business (an increase of 25% in net profit).

Now, let's get crazy and assume you increase your prices by 10%. Your income statement would look like this:

Revenue	$550,000
Cost of Goods Sold	(250,000)
Gross Profit	$300,000
Overhead	(150,000)
Net Profit	**$150,000**

A total profit increase of $50,000 (a 50% increase)!

"Now wait a minute," you might be saying. "My customers aren't dumb. If I raise my prices, some of them are going to use the Internet, the telephone, or some other resource to find a business to sell them what I sell at a cheaper price."

Maybe.

In fact, it's quite likely that some customers *will* decide to leave over a price increase. Before you hit the panic button, however, take a look at the impact a loss of some customers could have on Gross Profit.

Let's assume that 20% of your customers decide to leave over the price increase. That means that one out of every five customers stops buying from you.

Yikes!

Here's what your income statement would look like, after you increase prices by 10%, and had 20% of your customers decide to leave:

Revenue	$440,000
Cost of Goods Sold	(200,000)
Gross Profit	$240,000
Overhead	(150,000)
Net Profit	**$ 90,000**

Hah! "I win" you might be gloating. The 10% price increase makes the business $10,000 worse off. But don't be so quick to judge. Let's think a bit harder about whether things really would be worse or not.

SOME THOUGHT-PROVOKING QUESTIONS

That kind of thinking—the "I'm $10,000 Worse Off If I Raise Prices" attitude—misses some very important considerations. It's the "old-school," traditional, linear way of thinking about business. And it is exactly that way of thinking that traps so many business owners in a rut, working harder and harder to just get by (or even fall behind) and not having any fun.

So before we assume the old way is better than this new tactic, let's broaden the view. Although the example does, indeed, show you are now worse off by $10,000, we've left the total overhead exactly the same. Keep this in mind as you ask yourself the following questions:

1. If one out of every five customers left the business over the 10% price increase, which ones (which quadrant of the Customer Profitability Map) do you think they'd be most likely to come from?

Of course there is no way to know for sure in advance. But experience indicates that the majority of customers who would leave would likely be from your *Avoid!* quadrant.

Remember, those people are the ones who are your least profitable *and* have the lowest Resonance Scores. So good riddance to them!

2. If your customer volume dropped by 20%, would your overhead stay exactly the same, or would it drop?

It might stay the same, at least for the short-term. But if your customer volume dropped by 20% and stayed there, it's pretty certain that your overhead would decrease over time. And the decrease in overhead would go a long way (maybe all the way) toward offsetting the $10,000 net profit decrease shown above.

3. If your customer volume dropped by 20%, what could you and your team do with the extra time and resources?

It's very unlikely that you would just sit around (although you could, if that's what you wanted to do). Instead, you could use that entire extra day each week (because that's the effect losing 20% of your customers would have) to identify, connect with, and attract specific customers who would fit nicely into your *Target More* quadrant.

This would, in turn, increase your profit significantly, because these new customers would be ones who were highly profitable and who really connected with your business (high Resonance Scores).

Based on my actual experience over the years, I can almost guarantee that you would quickly find that, with the time freed by the 20% customer defection (most, if not all, of whom were in your *Avoid!* quadrant, anyway), you would spend more time serving your remaining clients and attracting new ones you liked (for your *Target More* quadrant).

The end result (I can't guarantee it, but I've seen this so many times, it's as close to a "sure thing" as you can get) would likely be:

- More sales to remaining customers (you'll finally have the time to find out what else they want and what else you can do for them)

- More customers, of the right type, to replace the ones that left

- More profit, fun, and free time

YOUR FOUND MONEY REPLACEMENT FACTOR

To drive this point home and make an abstract concept more concrete, I've created something I call the Found Money Replacement Factor (FMRF). The FMRF is a number that tells you, for any anticipated combination of price increase and customer defection rate, how many new customers you would need to attract to maintain the same overall gross profit you had before the customer defections.

The FMRF table for a business with a product that has a Gross Margin of 50% is shown in Exhibit 12.1 (you can check out the Found Money section of my Web site at www.stevewilkinghoff. com for additional tables for different gross margins).

		Price Increase (%)				
		5%	10%	15%	20%	25%
	5%	N/A	N/A	N/A	N/A	N/A
	10%	10%	N/A	N/A	N/A	N/A
	15%	40%	N/A	N/A	N/A	N/A
	20%	55%	15%	N/A	N/A	N/A
Attrition Rate (%)	25%	64%	32%	8%	N/A	N/A
	30%	70%	43%	23%	7%	N/A
	35%	74%	51%	34%	17%	6%
	40%	78%	58%	43%	28%	18%
	45%	80%	62%	49%	36%	27%

Exhibit 12.1 Found Money Marketing Replacement Factor (50% Gross Margin).

So here's how the table works.

You can ignore the shaded boxes. All they mean is that the particular combination of price increase and customer attrition would result in an increased gross profit for the business, even without attracting a single customer to replace any of those who left over the price increase.

Assume you're going to increase your prices by 15%, and that you are wondering what will happen if that increase results in 35% of your current customers leaving. Of course, it's very unlikely you would lose more than one-third of your customers, but let's run with this example to see how the table works. Going across the top row until you find the column for a 15% price increase, you then go down the column until you hit the row for a 35% attrition rate. You will notice the FMRF shows a value of 34%.

This is a pretty cool thing, if I do say so myself. It means that, given the planned 15% price increase and the anticipated 35% customer attrition rate, you would need to replace 34% of those who left to have the same total Gross Profit as before the price increase. In other words, you would only need to find roughly one new customer for every three who decided to leave over the price increase. Read that again: *you would only need to replace one out of every three customers who left to have the same total Gross Profit*.

The FMRF table can also be used to do some quick "mental tests" on the impact of any price increase you are contemplating. For example, if you are thinking about raising prices by 10%, you can use the FMRF table to get some comfort on how "risky" this tactic might be. Going across the top row until you get to the 10% Price Increase column, and then going down, you will notice something quite interesting. Up to and including an attrition rate of 15%, your total Gross Profit will actually increase (grey boxes)—even without adding any new customers! That means that it's only once you lose more than 15% of your existing customers that you even have to worry about replacing them with new customers to maintain the same Gross Profit.

If you feel that a 10% increase is due (maybe you haven't raised prices for several years out of fear—shame on you), you can get a lot of comfort by knowing that more than 15% of your customers will have to decide to leave *before you even need to START worrying about finding new customers to replace the gross profit you've lost!* Ask yourself how realistic you feel it is that you would lose more than 15% of your customers over that price increase. If you don't think it's very likely, you can confidently implement the price increase without worrying about suffering any negative consequences. And if you aren't sure if 15% or more would leave, set up a test and find out.

You can download worksheets to calculate your own Found Money Replacement Factor from the Found Money section of my Web site at www.stevewilkinghoff.com.

STEP TOWARD YOUR FEAR OF PRICING

It's a recurring phenomenon that the people who have the biggest problem dealing with price (and price increases) are business owners themselves. In almost every situation I have seen over the years, it's not the customers who have the biggest problem with prices—it's the business owners.

Price is always a consideration, there's no doubt about it. You can't simply charge any price at all and expect customers to accept it. You also can't take advantage of people and charge them high prices without providing them with enough value for a fair exchange.

This issue has been researched quite a lot in recent years. Here's one of my favorite studies that shows who has the biggest problem with price. This study was done to try to find out why customers left a business and what role pricing had in the customer's decision to leave. The study asked *consumers* what factors were a reason they left a company for a competitor. There were seven different factors from which they could pick.

The study also asked actual *companies* the same question. It asked them to cite the reasons *they felt* customers left their company for a competitor.

Exhibit 12.2 contains a quick summary of the answers that were given.

	Customer	Company	Gap
Customer Service	73%	21%	−52%
Needs Changed	9%	35%	26%
Convenience	9%	15%	6%
Functionality	13%	14%	1%
Price	25%	48%	23%
Quality	31%	17%	−14%
Other	15%	17%	2%

From Bob Thompson, "The Loyalty Connection: Secrets To Customer Retention and Increased Profits." © 2005 RightNow (www.rightnow.com).

Exhibit 12.2 Results from "The Loyalty Connection" survey.

Interesting findings, aren't they?

They show that almost half (48%) the businesses surveyed believed they lost customers primarily because of pricing. In other words, they thought roughly one out of every two customers who left their business for a competitor did it because of price issues.

But the reality (looking at the customer responses) was that only one in four left because of pricing. It wasn't nearly as big an issue for customers as the owners thought it was.

What's the impact of this misconception?

The most common impact is the refrain, "We can't raise our prices, or we'll lose customers." That statement is true. If you raise prices, your *will* lose some customers. But as the study shows (and actual experience over the years shows the same thing) it won't be nearly as many customers as the business owner thinks. In fact, based on the survey results, only half the number of customers the owners believed were lost due to price issues actually left for that reason). Business owners thought they lost customers over pricing about half the time. But the customers (the actual people who decided to switch) said price was a factor only one quarter of the time (25%).

This means that for every 100 customers a business loses, the owners *incorrectly* assume that 48 of those customers left due to pricing. But the truth is that only 25 of them left for that reason. In other words, the business owner would incorrectly assume price was the issue is 23 cases where it was not.

And making assumptions that are wrong by that much will likely cause the business owner to make some absolutely *terrible* business decisions.

For example, this wrong assumption could cause the owner to engage in price-reduction efforts, sacrificing a satisfactory margin and leading to competitive and operational problems—while also sacrificing the ability of the business to innovate, thrive, and compete.

Let's put some numbers to this example to see how big an impact that one "little" misconception could have.

Assume a business has 500 customers who buy twice a year, and spend $250 each time (with a 50% Gross Margin). The owner would like to increase prices by 10%, but has resisted (in fact, she hasn't raised her prices for three years now).

Her reluctance to raise prices has been costing her $25,000 per year ($25 per sale, to 500 customers twice a year). And since she has avoided this increase for three years, the true cost to her is a total lost profit of $75,000!

That's not chump change! It's a *huge* pile of money that was simply left lying on the table or thrown away.

Now let's return to the FMRF Table for this example. We will then be able to see what impact that price increase might have from that viewpoint.

Following across the top row until we get to the "10% Price Increase" column, and then going down the column, we note that she could lose up to 15% of her customers and still be better off by making that price increase. Based on a total of 500 customers, the business owner would be able to lose up to 75 of them before she would have to worry about replacing them to maintain the same Gross Profit.

But would she lose 75 of her customers? Would she lose more? We can't know for sure.

But the research findings shown above certainly indicate that most of her customers aren't as concerned about her prices as they are about other things. The research shows her customers care more about service and quality. That means there's a high probability that she wouldn't lose anywhere near 75 customers from the 10% price increase.

Another finding of the research was that business owners believed they only lost customers about 21% of the time due to customer service issues. However, customers rated it as an important issue in deciding to leave a company almost three-quarters of the time (73%).

So for every 100 customers who left a company, almost 75 of them left over customer service issues. But as the research shows, the business owner would think that only 21 of those defectors left because of customer service. In other words, the owner would incorrectly assume customer service was *not* an issue 54 times out of 100 cases, when it really *was* the issue. Kind of like a "false positive."

This grossly mistaken assumption would lead the business owner to act as though the real problem was either a price issue or simply the customers' changing needs. And once again, the business would be traumatized by a dangerously incorrect assumption.

The usual result of this kind of mistaken assessment is that the business owner falsely attributes the loss of customers to "big-box retailers," competition over the Internet, the economy, or any number of other pricing-related woes.

Naturally, the owner is determined not to lose these customers' business (and his or her livelihood). So they jump into action. But their action is based on incorrect assumptions, mistaken beliefs, and "gut feel" rather than well-reasoned thought and careful analysis (but not you, you Found Money Reader).

The sad result is that the owner usually decides to reduce prices and launch a marketing campaign to bring new people into their business.

But think about the result of those actions for a moment. What kind of customer are price-focused tactics most likely to attract?

Think back to the four quadrants of the Customer Profitability Map. Are they likely to be *Target More* customers? No way. The odds are extremely high that the vast majority of the new customers attracted in that manner will be flighty. They will tend to have very little loyalty to the business and aren't likely to be very profitable (they were attracted by low prices, after all).

The end result is that the business attracts low-profit clients who tend to have very low Resonance Scores (customers who fall into the *Avoid!* quadrant of the Customer Profitability Map). The business becomes plugged up with a lot of activity doing low-profit work. And that chokes off cash flow, prevents the owner and the team from achieving their best work, and creates a situation that only get worse over time.

YOUR FOUND MONEY PRICE CUT FACTOR

Now let's look at another set of numbers that are meant to show how much a business really gains by cutting prices.

We are a going to look at a metric I call the Found Money Price Cut Factor (FMPCF). This is similar to the Found Money Replacement Factor (FMRF) we covered earlier. The FMPCF is a measure of how large an increase in sales revenue is needed to offset a price decrease.

As a bit of foreshadowing, consider the very term *price cut*. Cuts on the human body are painful, dangerous, and sometimes even deadly. They don't call them price *cuts* without a reason.

Exhibit 12.3 is a chart showing the FMPCF.

		Price Cut (%)						
		5%	10%	15%	20%	25%	30%	35%
	20%	33%	100%	300%	N/A	N/A	N/A	N/A
	25%	25%	67%	150%	400%	N/A	N/A	N/A
	30%	20%	50%	100%	200%	500%	N/A	N/A
	35%	17%	40%	75%	133%	250%	600%	N/A
Gross Margin (%)	40%	14%	33%	60%	100%	167%	300%	700%
	45%	13%	29%	50%	80%	125%	200%	350%
	50%	11%	25%	43%	67%	100%	150%	233%
	55%	10%	22%	38%	57%	83%	120%	175%
	60%	9%	20%	33%	50%	71%	100%	140%

Exhibit 12.3 Found Money Price Cut Factor.

So what does the FMPCF do? It shows you, for any combination of price reduction and Gross Margin, what percentage increase in sales volume is needed *to simply have the same total Gross Profit as BEFORE the price cut.*

The shaded boxes that are marked N/A are situations where the price cut is so drastic that there is no possible way any increase in volume can make up for the price decrease. Basically, these situations occur when a price cut drops the selling price below the direct costs—Gross Margin becomes negative. As silly as it seems to cut prices to a level below what it costs to create a product or service, there are cases where business owners have tried this technique in an effort to stay competitive. And as you might expect, it simply doesn't work.

Let's examine an example of the FMPCF in action. Suppose a business owner has been losing a few customers lately and is convinced it's due to lower-priced competitors eroding market share. Based on the research study discussed earlier, you know that the owner's conviction about pricing is probably wrong. It's most likely customer service, remember?

Let's also assume the business in question has a current gross margin of 40%.

The owner is scared and worried about having the entire business disappear because of price competition. That (unfounded and irrational) fear leads the owner to cut prices by 10%. This seems to be a real-life, common, knee-jerk reaction of business owners who want to fend off perceived price competition.

Follow across the top row of the FMPCF table until you get to the column with 10% at the top of it. Then follow down the column until it intersects the row for a gross margin of 40%.

The number you find in that spot is 33%.

This tells you that you will need to increase your sales volume by 33% (a one-third increase!) to offset the effect of the price decrease, and leave you the same place you began.

Let this sink in for a moment, and then I'm going to ask you a question . . .

Does cutting your price by 10% look like a good strategy now? *Absolutely not!*

In fact, it's most likely an absolutely *terrible* business decision. Let's look at the bigger picture to see why.

- The business has been losing some customers over what the owner *believes* are price issues.

- Research shows that usually, when business owners *think* customers are leaving because of price, it's *actually* due to customer service or quality issues.

- The owner hasn't done any analysis to find out where those customers who did leave fall on the Customer Profitability Map. If they're in the *Avoid!* quadrant, who cares? It's actually a great thing that they're gone!

- The mistaken belief that price is the issue and the resultant reactive price cuts are most likely *not* going to do anything to stop customers from leaving—because the reason they are leaving is most likely *not* price.

- This means the business will probably continue to lose customers.

- And if that's the case, there's really no possible way the business will be able to actually increase volume by 33%. The price cut will do nothing but make the total Gross Profit of the business slide even further.

- Even if the owner did manage to increase sales volume by 33%, such a large spike in activity is probably going to force the owner to have to work much, much harder. After all, the 33% increase in activity only generates the same Gross Profit as *before* the price cut. That means there won't be any additional money from all that increased activity to hire more team members or increase infrastructure. Working one-third harder for the same amount of money is a sucker's bet—one you never want to get trapped into making.

So to summarize, there are a number of things that have combined into a "perfect storm" in this example:

- A wrong assumption about customers being lost due to price

- A failure to determine whether the customers who left are worth keeping by analyzing where they are on the Customer Profitability Map

- Knee-jerk price cuts

- An increased volume of activity (if the price cuts actually work) with no additional profit

And all those things were set in motion by the business owner's failure to understand their FMPCF. The end result is that the business is *worse off* after the price cuts and the subsequent chain of events than it ever was before the price cuts!

AARRRRGGGH! These scenarios (and they are quite common in real-life business situations) just completely drive me *nuts*! Those kinds of actions create a lot of financial and emotional hardship (and often bankruptcy) for so many business owners and their families.

And it's so preventable. All it takes is an understanding of the impact of price cuts and reference to a simple tool such as the FMPCF.

PRICE DOESN'T REALLY MATTER AT ALL!

Price, as you now know, is the number-one place to create huge gains in the profitability of your business. Any price increases multiply your profits like magic (remember what you learned earlier in this book?). And the profit impact of a price increase is almost assured to exceed any amount of profit lost from the few customers who decide to leave.

You now also know how foolish it is to reduce your prices as a tactic to gain customers to try to grow a business. The fact is that, in most cases, it is nearly impossible to achieve the level of sales increase needed to replace the lost profit caused from a price cut.

But despite the fact that it's far less scary to increase prices now that you understand your Found Money Replacement Factor (FMRF) and Found Money Price Cut Factor (FMPCF), there is still a bit of an art to raising your prices effectively.

It's true that you can probably simply increase your prices by 5–10% immediately, because it's likely you haven't raised your prices in a while. But to really create a business that maximizes its profit potential, you will probably need to raise prices even higher. At least, that should be a goal of yours.

That might be a real change in mindset for you. You may still be held back by the belief that customers will only pay so much. And that's true. They will only pay so much. But how much they will actually pay has nothing at all to do with your prices.

In fact, customers *never* buy *anything* because of the price.

When it comes to any purchase transaction, each potential buyer makes their decision without regard to price itself (don't worry, I haven't lost it—stay with me and you will see). But obviously, people do make decisions about whether or not to spend their money to buy something. So what do they base that buying decision on?

Value.

That's what really matters to any customer. They buy something if they feel they are getting enough value relative to the price.

What is value?

The easiest way to define it is by a "mathematical" formula that is very useful for helping think about your business.

The formula is this:

$$\text{Value} = \frac{\text{Perceived Benefits Received}}{\text{Price Paid}}$$

And that makes sense, doesn't it?

It's this formula that explains why people willingly pay between \$3–5 for a coffee at Starbucks when they could get a cup of coffee for a lot less almost anywhere else they went (in fact, they could often get their coffee for free at the office). And some of those cheaper places probably have a cup of coffee as good or better than the Starbucks brew.

But people still happily pay Starbucks their price (and hey, I'm one of those people, so I'm not pointing fingers, just making a point). They do it because they are getting more perceived benefits (caffeine buzz, flavor, convenience, a cool ambience, etc.) than the price they pay.

If the value formula for any transaction produces a number greater than 1.0, from the customer's viewpoint, the customer is likely to buy. After all, a value greater than 1.0 means the customer is receiving more perceived benefits than the price they are being asked to pay.

It's that "mental math" that's also behind the fact so many people spend money to buy bottled water. After all, they could get water for very low cost (or free if you're in a public place) from a tap or water fountain. If it was just about satisfying our thirst, we could carry around a bottle and refill it from a free public source while we were out.

If it wasn't for the value formula, and if price was the sole factor for making a purchase decision, bottled water companies wouldn't exist.

But there are a lot of bottled water companies. And people don't seem to take advantage of the free water options. They buy bottled water like crazy. For most people, the hassle of carrying a bottle from home, looking for someplace to fill it while out, and the uncertainty of the taste and quality of the water are too much. In other words, the perceived benefits of buying bottled water (convenience, it's cold, confidence in its quality, etc.) exceed the price.

And the price for bottled water is really, really high. My local store charges me about $1.50 for a little bottle of water. Some very quick calculations tell me I'm paying a lot more for that water than I am paying for fuel for my truck. Yet I complain about the high price of fuel and don't mention the even higher price for bottled water.

It's the value equation at work.

Your Customer Profitability Map (Again)

Think about your Customer Profitability Map (CPM) again for a few minutes. Can you use the value equation to explain why it's so important to create, analyze, and understand your CPM?

Do you understand why it's critical to the success of your business (and your dream lifestyle) for you to focus on only attracting customers who fit into your *Target More* quadrant?

Customers with a high Resonance Score are almost always getting more value from your business than ones with a low Resonance Score. The reason is that if they really connect with your business, your style, and your concepts, they will feel great about doing business with you. Don't underestimate the power of that fact. That forms part of the total perceived benefits they get from buying your products and services.

Therefore, the higher a customer's Resonance Score, generally the higher perceived benefits they will receive from your business. That means they will get more value, which allows for a higher price. And that makes for more profitable customers, products, and services.

Benefits, Not Features

A lot of really excellent information is readily available that goes deeply into using benefits over features in the sales process. And while you may not perceive your role as "selling," it's probably a large part of what you do. Selling is part of every interaction you and your team have with a customer. It is simply the process of trying to solve their problem by matching their needs to a product or service you sell that can help them.

Features are things that are "facts" about your products or services. They describe what your products and services are. Going back to our bottled water example, a feature is that the water is purified using reverse osmosis and state-of-the-art filters.

Features often create a trap for the business owner and their team. Because they have more knowledge and experience about their products, services, and industry than their customers have, owners and their team tend to take certain things for granted.

In the water example, the owner and team of a bottled water business *know* that the reverse osmosis process and their high-end filters are the best in the industry at removing heavy metals and potentially harmful bacteria (I'm just making this stuff up as an example; I'm not a water guru).

Because they know what it means (and what the benefit is) when someone mentions the words "reverse osmosis process", they assume everyone else knows exactly what it means too.

But the vast majority of people they come into contact with, most importantly their customers, don't know what the heck those things mean. Because the owner and team take that knowledge for granted, they don't specifically spell it out for their customer. That means the customers are forced to guess and assign some level of importance to those features. And they are not likely to assign the same level of importance to those features as the "experts" would—they don't really know enough about the product and industry.

Now let's discuss *benefits*. Benefits are what your products and services "do" for your customer.

This is often a tough mindset for many business owners to develop. It involves getting into the mind of your customer and thinking about what they are getting when they buy from you. Getting it right involves a lot of testing as well, Because what your customers consider a benefit is often not something you might have even imagined.

Your Features and Benefits

Now you're going to spend some time taking a hard look at your business, and each of your products and services.

This exercise should also be given to your team to get their input too. They will have different perspectives and fresh ideas that you might have missed.

Make several copies of the worksheet in Exhibit 12.4. Or you can go to the Found Money section of my Web site at www.stevewilkinghoff.com and download blank copies of the worksheet.

You're going to need one worksheet for each product and service your business sells, and each of your team members (assuming you decide to harness their talent, ideas, and expertise to help

Product/Service:	
Features	**Benefits**

Exhibit 12.4 Your features and benefits.

make this process even better) are going to need the same set of worksheets.

You should also make one for your overall business. This copy of the worksheet is to consider all the "global" things that permeate your entire business.

Identify the product or service at the top, and then list as many features of that product or service that you can come up with. In the column to the right, list one or more benefits for each of the features you identified.

Don't Force Your Customers to Buy Based on Price

Remember, customers buy value.

And looking at the value formula to refresh your memory, you will notice that the fewer perceived benefits a customer is getting from a transaction, the lower the price must be to make the sale (to create a value calculation of at least 1.0).

The problem occurs when there is an absence of clearly defined and described benefits for a customer. In that situation, the customer is forced to assess the perceived benefits based on what they know and what they can easily perceive. And that usually leaves them with no choice other than to rely on price to gauge the value they are getting from your business.

By not clearly identifying the benefits, and making sure your customer knows what those benefits are for your products and services, *you* are forcing your customer to use price as their buying criteria. *You* are making them buy on price. *You* are training your customers to be your own problem.

YOUR PRICE STRATEGY

Pricing is such a critical element to the success of your business and its ability to create money for you that it demands a lot of your attention. Yet paradoxically, most business owners don't give it *any* attention.

Pricing for your business isn't just something to think about. It isn't something to casually deal with. It is critical to the level of success and financial results your business achieves—so much so that it deserves its very own strategy. If you want to maximize your level of profit, cash flow, fun, and free time, you need to create a specific Price Strategy for your business.

A proper Price Strategy will take into account:

- What your customers really want

- What they really don't want

- How much Gross Profit your business needs to create to give you the financial and lifestyle results you want

Creating an effective Pricing Strategy requires you to work through several steps. It's usually a big help if you include your team in these steps, as well. After all, they are going to be on the front lines in the battle to implement your Pricing Strategy.

It's important that they understand the reasons behind your pricing and are given the opportunity to put their knowledge and creativity to work.

There are six steps in creating your Pricing Strategy.

Step One: Analyze the Current Situation

Figure out where your business is right now regarding its pricing. Are you a price taker? Or are you a price maker?

Use the worksheet in Exhibit 12.5 (you can also download copies from the Found Money section of my Web site at www.stevewilkinghoff.com) to compare your prices to those of your competitors.

Have one of your team members, or another person you know and trust, "shop" your competition. Either go into their business and find out what their prices are for products and services similar to yours, or phone and make the enquiries.

Step Two: Calculate Gross Margin for each Product / Service

What is the current Gross Margin for each of your main products or services?

What are the Gross Margin trends for the last three years for each of your main products or services? Brace yourself, because it

Competitor 1's Price				Our Price			
Product A	Product B	Product C	Product D	Product A	Product B	Product C	Product D

Exhibit 12.5 Pricing Strategy—competitive price analysis.

Gross Margin	Year 1	Year 2	Year 3
Product A			
Product B			
Product C			
Product D			

Exhibit 12.6 Pricing Strategy—Gross Margin analysis.

is often pretty demoralizing when you find a decreasing trend (but it's actually surprisingly, and sadly, common, so at least you've got company for now).

Use the worksheet in Exhibit 12.6 (or download it from the Found Money section of my Web site at www.stevewilkinghoff. com) to record data on your gross margin trends for the last three years.

Step Three: Do a PSWOT

A PSWOT is simply a traditional SWOT analysis (Strengths, Weaknesses, Opportunities, and Threats) applied specifically to the *pricing* of your business (hence the "P" in PSWOT).

Again, use the brainpower and input from your team to help do this exercise. They will have different information and a different perspective than you do, and that's terrific, because it makes the information you gather that much richer and more dynamic.

When filling out the boxes in each quadrant of your PSWOT, keep in mind the following:

- Strengths are the advantages you have that are created by the structure or operations of your business and its processes.

- Weaknesses are disadvantages that are created by your structures, operations, and processes.

- Both Strengths and Weaknesses are things that are internal to your business. You (your business and your team) have created them.

- Opportunities are things that are external to your business that you could convert into a Strength.

- Threats are things that are external to your business, but that have the potential to become a Weakness, or hurt your business.

Use the diagram in Exhibit 12.7 (or download from the Found Money section of my Web site at www.stevewilkinghoff.com) to capture your PSWOT analysis.

Pricing Strengths	Pricing Weaknesses
Pricing Opportunities	Pricing Threats

Exhibit 12.7 Your PSWOT.

Step Four: Set Your Target

What total Gross Profit does your business need to achieve for you to fulfill your personal lifestyle goals and have the level of profit, cash flow, fun, and free time you want? Revisit the earlier material on your Found Money Overhead to help with this step if you need it.

Decide which of your products and services are going to be the most effective at getting you to that gross profit. After all, it's all about leverage: Your more profitable products will maximize Gross Profit while minimizing the time and effort required.

Step Five: Develop Your Tactics

Decide which methods, techniques, and actions you are going to take to move your business toward the targets you have set.

Decide how many customers and how many of each product or service your business must sell to achieve those goals.

Step Six: Take Action, Measure the Results, and Compare to Targets

Continually measure the actual results you are achieving and compare them to your targets. You don't want to wait for half a year, three months, or even a month to go by before you realize that your tactics are missing their targets.

Success in implementing your Pricing Strategy requires you to try different tactics and techniques to continually try to improve your Gross Profit. Higher Gross Profit is created by selling products and services with high Gross Margins. And this requires you to ask your customers different questions, offer them things in different ways, interact with them differently, and continually try a stream of new variations.

Then you can keep any variations that result in improvements and discard those that don't. The best way to achieve quick improvement is to continually (at least weekly) measure your actual Gross Margins and sales mix to your targets.

Otherwise, it may take years, instead of months, to move toward your targets. And that's going to cost you a ton of lost profit and cash flow in the meantime—profit that you're *never* going to be able to get back. It's going to be lost forever, until you capture it.

CHAPTER

13

THE END OF THE LINE ...
AND JUST THE BEGINNING

So now what?

You've now filled your mind with an awareness of the amazing potential that's hidden inside your business ... the potential for it to do amazing things, to be transformed, to become a vehicle that serves your dream lifestyle and enables you to live your life your way, in your time.

As with all things in life, and like all the other business owners who have started their journey before you, you must take the first step. And that first step is for you to make some changes in how you and your business relate to each other, as well as some changes in how your business fits into your life, and the things that get done inside it.

This first step requires you to step back and take a hard (and honest) look at your business in its current state. Be completely honest with yourself about where *you* want your dream lifestyle to take you.

With that as a starting point, you can start to identify the gaps between the current position of your business (and lifestyle), and the position you'd like them to achieve. Those gaps will start to form the basis of your Found Money Roadmap, which will serve as your guide to transform your business.

Your business should be your willing, obedient, and able servant—a vehicle that sets you, your family, and your loved ones free to pursue your dream lifestyle and live your life at the level you truly desire.

That's possible when you apply the knowledge, skills, and tools that you have learned about in this book and on the Found Money section of my Web site at www.stevewilkinghoff.com.

Make the commitment to yourself to get control of your business and to make it your servant in living the life of your dreams.

Don't just close this book and think about what you have learned. Make the effort to *act* on what you have seen and learned, and your life and business will never be the same again.

As my friend Michael Gerber of *The E-Myth, Revisited* fame says,

When you hear something, you forget it.

When you see something, you remember it.

But not until you **do** something will you understand it.

So please take that first step. The step of doing.

Steve Wilkinghoff, C.A., is the founder, chairman, and CEO of BizDog Strategic Business Solutions Inc., which provides business owners and managers with the help they need to truly understand the financial side of their business and teaches them how to proactively create the financial results their dream lifestyle demands. Steve has been referred to as an innovative thinker and a visionary when it comes to the role traditional "accounting information" should have in helping business owners and managers succeed. Steve consults with clients around the globe, and delivers seminars and corporate presentations anywhere there is a need and demand.

Steve's company, BizDog Strategic Business Solutions Inc., is rapidly developing a worldwide reputation for its innovative and effective systems, training, and resources. Its proprietary technology and innovative thinking have led other businesses and consultants to seek out both Steve and his company to help them deliver world-class solutions to their clients.

If you are interested in having Steve Wilkinghoff address your organization, present at your function, or consult with your business, or if you wish to receive more information about his innovative Found Money system, books, tapes, and consulting, call BizDog Strategic Business Solutions Inc. at 403-528-4241, or visit us at www.stevewilkinghoff.com.